Cockermouth Amateur Theatre

A PICTORIAL HISTORY

FRONT COVER PICTURE: The chorus line from Cockermouth Operatic Society's production
of **'Tonight's the Night'** L-R: *Mabel Sisson, Laura Harrison, Freda Sharp,
Dorothy Birkett, Amy Tiffen* and *Doreen Tiffen.*

Published 2010 by *Little Bird Publications*

ISBN 978-0-9551845-2-9

Design by karensawrey.com

Printed in UK by Verité CM Limited (veritecm.com)

For Gill

Acknowledgments

This book has been made possible by the many contributions and the help of numerous individuals and organisations. With financial support from the Heritage Lottery Fund, the Cockermouth Museum Group spent countless hours researching, cataloguing and restoring the precious photographs contained in this collection. I am greatly indebted to those members, past and present, who gave their time so generously: *Eric Apperley, Ann Binns, Josephine Brown, Harold Burslem, Eric Cass, Gloria Edwards, Aline Elliott, Margaret Hubbard, Deborah Kitching, Janet Mansfield, Harold Martin, Lis Morris, Ted Petty, Barbara Ramsden* and *Ena Robinson.*

Others, not connected to the Museum Group, also supported the project by either directly contributing to this publication or by assisting with funding, research, design, editing and publicity. Especial thanks in this respect go to: *Melvyn Bragg, Phil Campbell, Hunter Davies, Kate Hilton, Janet Nixon, Karen Sawrey, Nick Stanley* and *Janet Thompson.*

There are many others with past connections to the Cockermouth Amateur Operatic Society, WEA Players, Drama Group, the All Saints' Pantomime Company, Sadie Cussons' Dance School and CADS, who generously loaned photographs, shared memories or helped in many other ways with this project. They include: *John Barker, Brian Wilkinson, Sylvia Hansford, Mabel Hefford, Dorothy Hewitt, Sylvia Lawrence, Rosalind Pontin, Jacqueline Smith, Jean Todhunter, Derek Barratt, Margaret Brown, Joan Cavaghan, Nelson Chicken, Barbara Cunliffe, Lola Foster, Barbara Goodfellow, Peter Hodgson, Geof Hool, Diana James, Alice Marley, Bob Pritchard, Mike Rooney, Edna Sinclair, Ann Teasdale, Elizabeth Tinker, Betty Turner, Ian Walker, Alice Bishop, Jan Dockwray, Hannah Evans, Liz Fitton, Stewart Grant, Mike Palmer, Simon Pollitt, Jill Roper* and *Len Wainwright.*

And, of course, thanks are also due to the many photographers without whom a book like this would not have been possible. Unfortunately, as the majority of photographs were sourced from family scrap books it has not been possible to trace and credit each of them. However, some of the photographs will have been professionally taken and are reproduced here by courtesy of Ivor Nicholas and Cumbria Newspapers Limited.

Greg Greenhalgh
Papcastle. July 2010

Cockermouth Amateur Theatre

A PICTORIAL HISTORY
by Greg Greenhalgh

Cockermouth Museum Group

*To Anne
with best Wishes
Greg Greenhalgh*

Little Bird Publications

Foreword by Hunter Davies

There can't be many towns, or even villages, that haven't got an amateur dramatic or musical society, with ordinary people casting aside their every day work and worries to live out their fantasies and tread the boards, or simply to improve their social life, meet other people, take part in a communal and community activity.

I have never acted in such groups myself, and last trod the boards in a Carlisle Grammar School production of 'She Stoops to Conquer' in the 1950s. I played the violin, very, very badly, in a crowd scene. Didn't even have a speaking part. But I like to feel I am intimately connected with

CADS, as a supporter of their efforts, and also as a client of Beryl, every time I go into Cockermouth to get my hair cut. I don't actually know Beryl's surname, but I always use her hair salon in the middle of town. She is clearly a stalwart of the society and regales me on every visit with a blow by blow account of the latest play she is rehearsing, the background dramas and tensions, the details of her part, and of course how sometimes it was not the part she wanted. Much better than discussing the weather.

There can't be many people in these am-dram groups who have

not kept a scrap book of photos, newspaper cuttings and the theatre programmes of their experience 'treading the boards'. These scrap books provide a valuable source of social history and over the last fifteen years, the Museum Group in Cockermouth has built up a collection of such memorabilia which provide a commentary on the plays, musicals and operas staged in the town for more than 150 years.

The museum's photographic history starts in the early 1900s with the All Saints' Church Group. I can look at this photograph for hours, not just because of the amazing costumes, but studying

the faces, trying to identify any of their descendants today. Then during World War I there are some photographs of 'Betty Wilson Dandy Coons' fund raising efforts supporting the troops. Not quite the sort of thing we would approve of today, but at one time, such concert parties were found all over the country.

In common with all the am-dram groups, the societies in Cockermouth have been, and still are, part of the social fabric of the town. The tradition of local people coming together in their own free time to collectively create entertainment for their community has gone on from generation to generation. Typically these groups involve whole families and the same names can often be seen spanning many years. Lifelong friendships are formed within these groups and sometimes marriages too. But what happens when the curtain falls after the last performance? The audience return home happily entertained and the memories stay vivid amongst those who were involved in the show. But even these memories will fade in time.

By publishing a pictorial history of these shows, generations to come can get a glimpse into the life of their parents and grandparents in Cockermouth.

But the book is also valuable as social history, of interest to anyone, anywhere, reflecting the changing fashions in amateur dramatics, local theatres, costumes, choices of plays and other entertainments over the last 100 years.

Hunter Davies
Loweswater, March 2009

▷ Hunter Davies

1906

Stage plays have been performed in Cockermouth for centuries, but this photographic history starts in 1906 with the All Saints' Church Group production of **The Gitane**.

Various hotels and public rooms in the town have been used for theatrical performances. The Sun Inn and Posting House in Market Place dates back to the mid 18th Century and is one of the oldest theatrical venues in Cockermouth. The inn had a theatre at the rear of the premises and the earliest records traced relate to a performance there in 1775 by the famous actor and literary figure, Thomas Holecroft. The Cockermouth Museum Group have an advertising bill from a 1854 production at the Sun Inn, staging four one-act plays: the tragedy, **Jane Shore**, the farce, **Supper For Five**,

the comedy, **John Bull**, and the farce, **The Captain Is Not A Miss!** In the 20th Century the Sun Inn served for a time as the British Legion Club before becoming an antiques shop in the late 1980s and then extensively renovated and opened as the '1761' wine bar in 2008.

The Globe Hotel in the main Street was also an important coaching inn from the early 18th to mid 19th Century. Its first floor ballroom survives and in 1851 the Cockermouth Philomusical Society staged a concert there. The hotel's ballroom was a regular venue for touring professional drama in the 20th Century and in the late 1980s, Cockermouth's current amateur drama group, CADS, also staged all their plays there.

The Royal Assembly Rooms were opened in the 1860s on the site in Crown Street, converted to Anderson Court in the 1990s. The Assembly Rooms had an audience capacity of approximately 1,000 and in 1879, a 'new amateur company', the Cockermouth Entertainment Society (later known as the 'Cockermouth Amateur Dramatic Club'), played a double bill there: **All a Hoax** and **The Virginia Mummy**. This group staged many plays in and around the town in the years leading up to World War I and some of their members became principals of the 'Cockermouth Operatic & Dramatic Society' in the 1920s.

The earliest Cockermouth amateur performance traced is a group in 1849 who appeared on New Year's Day in the Theatre Loyal, Rubby

Banks, performing **The Drama of Charles II** (or The Merry Monarch) and the laughable farce, **The Merry Wags of Windsor**. This was an all male company, the ladies of the piece being played by gentlemen!

Plays, operas and musical concerts were also regularly staged in the Apple Tree Hotel on Main Street (now the Wordsworth Hotel), the Public Hall in Station Street (demolished in 1974 to make way for the National Westminster Bank), the Freemasons' Hall in Challoner Street and the Drill Hall on Castlegate Drive (built in 1886 and converted into a Sports Centre in the late 1980s).

▷ All Saints' Church Group **The Gitane** 1906

1906

1913

△ Construction of the Grand Theatre in 1913

The Grand Theatre in Station Road, was designed by Henry Irving Graham, and opened to the public just before the outbreak of World War I. The theatre had a seating capacity of 600 and staged a wide variety of entertainment including drama, opera, orchestral concerts, choir recitals, variety shows, silent films, cinema and finally bingo.

Arthur Wilson was the theatre manager in the 1920/30s and it is from the scrapbooks of his sister, Lizzie Wilson, that much of the material in the early part of this book was sourced. Miss Wilson was the founding secretary of the Cockermouth Amateur Operatic Society and, from its inception in 1920, she kept a marvellous archive of photos, theatre programmes and newspaper cuttings.

GRAND THEATRE

VETERINARY SURGERY

1913

△ The former Grand Theatre photographed in 2009

1916

During World War I, Lizzie Wilson established The Dominoes Concert Party. The group performed in and around Cockermouth during the war and raised £600 for patriotic parcels for the soldiers in the trenches (equivalent to more than £25,000 in today's money!).

1916

▷ The Dominoes 1918

◁ The Dominoes 1916

1916

'BETTY WILSON'S DANDY COONS'

1917

Lizzie Wilson's niece, Betty Wilson, also fronted a minstrel performing group. This photograph was taken at a fund-raising concert at Hames Hall, Cockermouth in July 1917. Betty Wilson is standing, second from the left of the picture, (wearing a top hat) next to Lizzie Wilson. Conducting is Elsie Ray, who later would go on to produce many of the plays for the Cockermouth WEA Players in the 1940s and 1950s.

△ **'Betty Wilson's Dandy Coons'** 1917. L-R Standing: *Lizzie Wilson, Betty Wilson, Miss B. Rennicks, Miss M. Allinson, Louise Hill* and *Miss H. Kirkbride*. Seated: *unidentified lady*, then: *Misses M.H. Banks, Laura Harrison, Moyra Fletcher, Elsie Ray, Mary Wilson, F. Ellwood, H. Senior* and *E. Elwin*.

1920

An inaugural meeting was held in All Saints' Church Rooms on 23rd September 1920, at which the Cockermouth Amateur Operatic Society was formed from the members of 'The Dominoes'.

Miss Alice Waugh of The Burroughs, in Papcastle, was to be the Society's first president and Vernon Turver the treasurer. The meeting declared that Mr Jonathan Huddart would act as the musical conductor and Miss Margaret Forbes-Wilson would direct their first production.

Jonathan Huddart was the society's musical director for every opera and musical they staged from 1921 to 1937. A local man, he was born in Crown Street, Cockermouth in 1872. He was the son of a blacksmith and came from a family strongly

associated with the Church. From an early age he was 'practically cradled in music', both his parents having excellent singing voices. He was officially recognised as a choir member of the Congregational Church Choir in 1879 when he was only seven. Before leading the Operatic Society, he had sung at concerts and in competitions in and around Cockermouth and had conducted choirs for the Harmonic Society, Congregational Church and Christy Minstrel troupe. He conducted a massed choir at the opening of the town's Harris Park in 1894 and at the unveiling of the War Memorial in 1920.

△ *Lizzie Wilson*, founding member of the Cockermouth Amateur Operatic Society

▽ *Jonathan Huddart*, Musical Director Cockermouth Amateur Operatic Society

Margaret Forbes-Wilson from Grange-over-Sands, was engaged as the society's Artistic Director (known then as 'Producer') and headed the company for both musicals and plays from 1921 to 1932. Always billed as *'Madame Forbes-Wilson - Late of the D'Oyly Carte Opera Company'*, she produced musicals and operas for societies in Whitehaven, Workington, Maryport and Cockermouth for almost thirty years - her first such production was in Whitehaven in 1905. She was described as *'something of a martinet'* who stood no nonsense. Although she directed her productions *'with a rigid firmness of purpose'*, she never lost the goodwill of her cast.

◁ *Madame Forbes-Wilson*

1921

△ **The Pirates of Penzance** cast photo 1921

1921

On the 4th May 1921 the curtain was raised in the Grand Theatre for Cockermouth Operatic Society's inaugural production of Gilbert & Sullivan's **The Pirates of Penzance**. The show ran for four nights with Jonathan Huddart in the leading role of the Pirate King.

The production had a cast of thirty four with Harry Dixon playing Major-General Stanley, John Huddart (Samuel), John Black (Frederic), Joseph Bell (the sergeant of police), Elsie Wilson, Joyce Graham, Miss N. McKay and Louise Hill in the roles of General Stanley's daughters and Miss A. Lowes as Ruth, 'pirate maid of all work'.

1922

One year later, in May 1922, the Operatic Society opened at the Grand Theatre with their second production. This time they staged Gilbert & Sullivan's lavishly costumed **Mikado** for a six-night run, plus matinee. The title role was played by John Huddart, with Elsie Wilson playing Yum Yum. John Black took the role of the Mikado's son, Nanki Poo, and Musical Director, Jonathan Huddart played Pooh-Bar 'The Lord High Everything'. John Campbell (seated on the left of the photo) led the twenty-one piece orchestra, which comprised of eight violins, two violoncellos, one contra bass, two flutes, one oboe, one clarinet, one bassoon, two cornets, one trombone, a piano and drums.

Special late trains returned theatre-goers from nearby Cockermouth Station to the neighbouring towns of Keswick and Workington.

In December 1922, a three act comedy, **Tilly of Bloomsbury** was staged on two nights at the Grand Theatre. The show's programme billed the performing company as the 'Cockermouth Amateur Operatic & Dramatic Society'. The play was produced by Madame Forbes-Wilson with a cast of sixteen actors. Gladys Grave played the title role alongside Mr F.L. Boreman in the part of her lover, Richard. Harry Dickson played Mr Stillbottle, Lizzie Wilson, Lady Mainwaring and Vernon Turver played Abel Mainwaring MP.

◁ *Harry Dickson* in the comic role of KoKo 'The Lord High Executioner', pleads fake love to Katisha, played by *Annie Lowes*, in a scene from **The Mikado**

△ **The Mikado** cast photo taken at the side of the Grand Theatre in 1922

1923

1923

Gilbert & Sullivan's **Patience** (or **Bunthorne's Bride**) was chosen as the Operatic Society's fourth production. The opera had a cast of thirty-eight and was again staged on six nights, plus a Saturday afternoon matinee, in May 1923, at the Grand Theatre. Elsie Moscrop was cast in the title role of **Patience**, Gladys Grave in the part of Lady Angela, Miss E. Hayton as Lady Ella, Mrs Lee as Lady Saphir, Mr W.G. Bryers as Bunthorne, Jonathan Huddart as Archibald Grosvenor and Miss A. Lowes as Lady Jane.

In December 1923, Madame Forbes-Wilson directed the society's drama wing in the comedy **All Of A Sudden Peggy** at the Grand Theatre. Gladys Grave was cast in the title role with a cast of eleven. Other principal parts were played by: Mr F.L. Boreman (Jimmy Kefpel), Vernon Turver (Lord Crackenthorp), Lizzie Wilson (Lady Crackenthorp), Miss E. Hayton (Mrs O'Mara), Willie Sharp (Major Phipps) and Frank Mitchell (Jack Menzies).

◁ **Patience** cast photo 1923
Front Row: *Mr F. Mitchell, Miss A. Mitchell, Miss K. Bell, Mr W. G. Byres, Miss D. Mitchell, Mr J. Campbell*
Second Row: *Mr A.J. Huddart, Miss G. Grave, Mr W. Sharp, Mrs Lee, Mr W. Trainer, Mrs Moscrop, Mr J.W. Huddart, Miss Hayton, Mr J. Black, Miss A. Lowes*
Third Row: *Misses S. Brash, L. Hill, M. Walker, M. Long, G. Cairns, L. Harrison, M. Mitchell, M. Dent, M. Jennings, M. Huddart, L. Wilson*
Back Row: *Messrs D. Wright, G. Hefford, M. Briggs, J. Bewsher, T. Lowes, T. Walker, V. Turver, A. Eland, J. Martin, E. Bewsher, F. Williamson, J. Moscrop.*

▷ *Elsie Moscrop* in the title role of **Patience** 1923

△ **The Gondoliers** cast photo 1924

1924

The Operatic Society chose another Gilbert & Sullivan production in the Grand Theatre in May 1924. **The Gondoliers** had a large cast of forty-seven, with Jonathan Huddart in one of the leading roles, that of Don Alhambra del Bolero, the Grand Inquisitor. Harry Dickson made a welcome return to the stage playing the comic part of the Duke of Plaza-Toro and Kathleen Rook made her début in a principal part, the Duke's daughter, Casilda. The local press praised her performance playing alongside Matthew Briggs (Luiz, the Duke's attendant).

In November, the society also staged a fund-raising concert, **A Café Chantant** in the Public Hall in Station Street.

△ Some of the cast of **Dorothy** in 1925 with Lord Leconfield's foxhounds

1925

In their fifth year, the Operatic Society finally moved away from Gilbert & Sullivan to stage the Stephenson-Cellier comic opera, **Dorothy**. At the matinee performance on the Saturday afternoon, thirty inmates from the Cockermouth workhouse were in the audience, by invitation of the society.

Hannah (Nan) Steele starred in the title role, **Dorothy**, with Mary Huddart playing her cousin, Lydia Hawthorne. Harry Dixon reportedly stole the show with his comic portrayal of the bibulous William Lurcher, but the highlight of the production was undoubtedly the appearance on stage of eight foxhounds from Lord Leconfield's West Cumberland Otter Hunt pack.

1926

The two-act musical comedy, **A Country Girl** was chosen for the Society's 1926 production. The show ran at the Grand Theatre from 26th April to 1st May and was again produced by Madame Forbes-Wilson. Nan Steele was again the leading lady and the show introduced a new principal, Freda Marshall in the role of Marjorie Joy.

1926

▷ *Freda Marshall* and *Nan Steele* in **A Country Girl** 1926

1926

△ The principals in **A Country Girl** 1926

1927

In 1927 the Cockermouth Amateur Operatic & Dramatic Society (now sometimes billed as CAOS) staged their annual musical, plus a three-act play. The comic opera **Florodora** was performed at the Grand Theatre in May, again produced by Madame Forbes-Wilson. For the third year in succession, Nan Steele was chosen as the leading lady, supported by Vera Mitchell. Other principal parts were played by Mary Huddart (Lady Holyrood), Harry Dickson (Anthony Tweedlepunch), Mr W. Trainer (Frank Abercoed), Mr H. Duffield (Cyrus W. Gilfain), Frank Entwistle (Captain Arthur Donegal) and Eric Bewsher (Leandro).

In November, the society staged a three act farce, **Are You A Mason** at the Grand Theatre. The twelve strong cast included Gilbert James as Frank Perry, Harry Dixon as Amos Bloodgood and Lizzie Wilson as Caroline Bloodgood.

△ **Florodora** chorus line up 1927

L-R Messrs *S. Jackson, G. Hefford, A.E. Faulkner, H. Scott, G. James, N. Mann.*

Misses *I. Mitchell, A. Tiffen, M. Bewsher, M. Dent, M. Mitchell, L. Harrison.*

1927

◁ **Florodora** female
chorus line 1927

△ **Florodora** - cast photo 1927

Back Row: *G. Hefford, A. Faulkner, D. Mitchell,*
J. Jackson, A. Taylor, M. Kirkbride, S. Graham,
W. Ewart, R. Sisson, H. Scott, G. James, N Mann.
Middle Row: *V. J. Turner, A. Millington,*
F. Williamson, M. Jennings, D. Bewsher,
L. Wilson, B. Kirkbride, R. Dallas, J.W. Huddart.
Second Row: *J Campbell I Mitchell,*
A Tiffen, M Bewsher Dolores, M Dent ,
M Mitchell, L Harrison
Front Row: *L. Hill, D. Ward, S. Grave,*
J. Graham, G. Watson, M. Mann, S. Cook.

1928

Nan Steele again played the title role in the Operatic Society's 1928 musical, **Miss Hook of Holland**. Gilbert James was cast in the lead role of Ludwig Schnapps, with the inimitable Harry Dixon as Mr Hook. Jonathan Huddart played Simon Slinks and Vernon Turver played Van Eck.

1928

▷ *Harry Dixon, Jonathan Huddart* and *Vernon Turver* in **Miss Hook of Holland** 1928

1928

△ **Miss Hook of Holland** cast photo 1928

In November 1928, Madame Forbes-Wilson staged a three-act farce, **Eliza Comes to Stay** at the Grand Theatre. There were nine characters in the piece. Gilbert James was in the lead role as the Hon. Sandy Verrall, supported by Sadie Grave in the role of Dorothy.

In 1928 Alida M. Lochead of the Workers Education Association, formed the Cockermouth WEA Players. The group performed in the gas lit basement of the old Wesleyan Chapel in Market Street.

▷ **Eliza Comes to Stay** - cast photo 1928.
Gilbert James (centre) played the
principal role of the Hon. Sandy Verrall

Built in 1841, the chapel became the Urban District Council offices in 1932, and later, Cockermouth Town Hall. Former WEA member, Hilda Banks, recalled how the group's electrician had to rig a cable across the River Cocker (on the right of the photo) to the basement of the chapel, to supply the power for the stage lights!

Their first production was **Dear Departed**, a comedy with a cast of six, written by Stanley Houghton in 1911. **Dear Departed** was followed by **The Price of Coal** and then **Shadow of the Glen** featuring Norah Burke, Helen Cooper, A. Tramp and Anthony Watson. In the 1940s and 1950s, Anthony Watson produced many of the plays for the Drama Society.

1928

△ Wesleyan Chapel in Market Street

▷ Built in 1841, the Wesleyan Chapel became the Urban District Council offices in 1932 and later Cockermouth Town Hall

1929

In May 1929 the Operatic Society staged the A.M. Willner / Robert Bodanzky musical comedy, **Gipsy Love** at the Grand Theatre. Mr W Trainer was cast in the leading role of Joszi, alongside Nan Steele who played Ilona.

Then in December, Madame Forbes-Wilson produced the Operatic Society's drama, **Paddy, the Next Best Thing** at the Grand Theatre. The four act play had a cast of fifteen. Sadie Grave was cast in the title role of Paddy Adair, with other leading parts taken by Mr I. Ricards (General Adair), Vera Mitchell (Eileen Adair), Mr L. Scott (Jack O'Hara) and Gilbert James (Lawrence Blake).

During this period, the Cockermouth WEA Players also staged the plays **Double Demon**, **Escape**, **The Skin Game**, **You Never Can Tell** and **Rising Sun** – production details, dates and venues unknown at time of publication.

◁ *Miss Steele & Mr W. Trainer* in **Gipsy Love** 1929

◁ *Sadie Grave*, Dance Teacher and Choreographer, arranged the dance sequences in **Gipsy Love** but was unable to appear in the actual performance due to illness.

△ Another scene from **Gipsy Love** 1929

1930

The Operatic Society's May, 1930 musical at the Grand Theatre was **The Toreador**, written by Ivan Caryll and Lionel Monckton. The show starred Mr W. Trainer in the title role of Carajola, a part in which, according to the West Cumberland Times, 'he acted superbly, and admirably portrayed the dignity and pride which the courage of a Toreador inspires.' Dona Teresa, the Toreador's betrothed, was played by Gladys Huddart and Gladys Watson played the widowed bride, Malton Hoppings, 'one of the favourites in the piece' said the reviewer in the West Cumberland Times. Harry Dickson's comic portrayal of Sammy Gigg again achieved significant accolades, particularly in his scenes with choreographer, Sadie Grave. Five members of Cockermouth's Mechanics Band were brought into the show to play in the on-stage marching band.

In the same year, the WEA Players staged **One Hundred Year's Old**, **Everyman of Every Street**, **The Man Who Wouldn't Go To Heaven** and **The Romantic Young Lady**.

△ **Toreador** 1930

△ **Toreador** 1930

1931

In 1931, the WEA Players staged **The Valiant**, **Point of View** and **The Tragedy of Man**. The cast of **The Valiant** included Molly Hodgson, John E Collins and Anthony Watson. Elsie Ray and Molly Hodgson starred in **The Tragedy of Man**. Elsie Ray, the proprietor of a millinery business in Main Street, was to become the mainstay of the WEA Players for nearly thirty years, producing many of their plays.

In the same year, the Operatic Society staged their annual musical plus a three act farce and two variety concerts. When the final curtain fell on their 1930 production of **The Toreador**, the society announced that they would be reverting back to the works of Gilbert & Sullivan in 1931. The announcement was 'greeted with loud applause!!!'

In May that year, they presented **Iolanthe** to packed audiences. The show starred Harry Dickson as the Lord Chancellor. His rendering of 'Faint heart never won fair lady' received no fewer than three encores. The West Cumberland Times reported his '…. *bringing forth roars of mirth with a dance of joy, the equal of which has never been seen on the Grand Theatre stage. Mr Dickson is obviously a player of experience. Bubbling over with humour he was in his element and found plenty of scope for his talent in delivering effectively the irresistibly witty sayings and parodies of the inimitable Gilbert.'*

▷ *Nan Steele* in **Iolanthe** 1931

1931

◁ *Maisie Bie* from Whitehaven

△ **HMS Optimists**

On 19th and 20th October 1931, the Operatic Society produced a three-act farce, **Lord Richard in the Pantry**. Gilbert James starred in the title role, with Mrs Turner, Chris Woodhouse, Duncan Pattinson and Alf Birkett in other principal roles. On the following night, Musical Director, John Campbell, presented an evening of Variety Entertainment in the Grand Theatre. Then in November 1931 Sadie Grave produced **Optimists** at the Grand Theatre. The company included Kitty Bell, Duncan Pattinson, Gladys Watson, Gladys Huddart, Rene Rydiard, Cecil Harris-Ward, Gilbert James, Chris Woodhouse, Alf Birkett, Billie Byres, Alec Wardle, Clarence Jeffries, Ivor Richards, Annie Rydiard, Tom Elliot, Bert Kirkbride, Joe Roe, George Bowman, Frank Williamson, Margaret Johnston, Amy Tiffen, Frank Entwistle, Leslie Huddart, Mary Bewsher, Laura Harrison, Freda Sharp, Edina Harris-Ward, Kitty Dent, Mary Mitchell, Annie Watson, Jean Mitchell and Eileen Scott. The 'surprise item' on the bill was the young ballerina, Maisie Bie, from Whitehaven – the author's mother!

△ **The Duchess of Dantzic** cast photo 1932

1932

In October 1932, on the opening night of the Operatic Society's autumn comedy play, the Group's Director, Madame Forbes-Wilson, died, aged 77, at the home of her sister, in London. She had produced eighteen operas, musicals and plays in Cockermouth over the last decade of her life.

1932

In April 1932, Madame Forbes-Wilson's final production, **The Duchess of Dantzic,** opened at the Grand Theatre. A young, local bank clerk, Tom Elliot, played the part of Napoleon Bonaparte. He was described in the local press as 'lean and brutal in appearance, beetling eyebrows, lock of hair down centre of forehead, deliberate gait, deep, ponderous voice, and never a smile.' The only criticism was of 'an unconvincing kiss' in the scene with Nan Steele (the Duchess, Madam Sans Gene) and Mr W. Trainer as Sergeant Francois Lefebvre. The press wanted to see 'more fervour in the kissing scene'! The cast of fifty-eight included Gladys Huddart, Jonathan Huddart, Frank Entwistle, Tom Elliot, Alf Birkett, Eric Bewsher and Gilbert James. The musical director was Jonathan Huddart and

Sadie Grave arranged the dances. The nineteen-piece orchestra was conducted by John Campbell.

In October 1932, the Operatic Society staged a four act comedy, **The Middle Watch** at the Grand Theatre with Gladys Huddart (Fay Heaton) and Sadie Grave (Mary Carlton) in the principal roles. The play had only opened in London's West End in 1929 and a cinema version had also been released. The show at the Grand Theatre cost £100 to stage, a budget in today's values in excess of £3,000!

During this time, the WEA Players also staged **The Theatre**, **The Three Wayfarers** and **Crime at Blossoms**.

▷ **The Duchess of Dantzic** 1932

1933

Tom Rawsthorn, from Ulverston, took over the reins in 1933 and directed the Operatic Society's next production at the Grand Theatre, a musical play, **The Street Singer**. Written by Frederick Lonsdale and Percy Greenbank, **The Street Singer** was a modern musical, which had opened at The Lyric Theatre in London in 1924.

Rehearsals took place in the Rampant Bull Hotel, opposite the Grand Theatre, and the show opened there in May 1933 with Kitty Bell in the title role and with Jim Huddart as Bonni. Ticket prices were 2s in the stalls and 3s 6d for a seat on the balcony. The profits of the show (£75) were once again donated to the Cockermouth Cottage Hospital.

In November 1933, Tom Rawsthorn directed the Operatic Society's drama wing in the thriller, **Bulldog Drummond**, at the Grand Theatre. The show starred Ivor Richards (the master crook, Carl Peterson), Gilbert James (in the title role of Captain Drummond), Irene Rydiard (Irma Petersen) and Gladys Huddart (as the heroine, Phyllis Benton). Also, around this time, the WEA Players staged the plays, **Nine Till Six**, **Capt Brassbound's Conversation** and **Symphony in Illusion**.

Nine Till Six featured Elsie Ray, Winnie Billington, Lillian Jeffries and Alma Clark.

△ **The Street Singer** 1933

▷ Artistic Director - *Tom Rawsthorn*

1934

△ **Tonight's the Night** chorus line 1934 L-R: *Annie Watson*, possibly *Betty Folder*, *Mabel Sisson*, possibly *Margaret Mitchell*, *Dorothy Chicken (nee Birkett)*, *Mary Mitchell*, *Nora Briggs* and *Doreen Tiffen*

elderly, hen-pecked husband, Montagu Lovitt-Lovitt), Nancy Stoddart (June), Kitty Bell (Beatrice Carraway), Irene Rydiard (Angela Lovitt-Lovitt), Tom Elliot (Dudley Mitten), Leslie Williamson (the tango teacher), Walter Deacon (Alphonse), Clarence Jeffries (Robun Carraway), Jock Hetherington (policeman), Alf Faulkner (Lord Ridgemont) and Betty Folder (as Daisy de Menthe)

Once again, the profits from the show were donated to the Cockermouth Cottage Hospital. Some £850 (approximately £25,000-£30,000 in today's values) had been contributed to the hospital by the Operatic Society since their formation in 1921.

In the same year, the WEA Players staged **The Whiteheaded Boy** with Tom Silvester, Elsie Ray, Anthony Watson and Winnie Billington. During this period they also performed **No Man's Island**, **A Long Xmas Dinner**, **Romany Road** and **Storm in Port**.

1934

Tom Rawsthorn directed his second musical for the society in April 1934 at the Grand Theatre. Doreen Kirkbride from Whitehaven was brought in to design the choreography, which included a ballet sequence. The show choice for 1934 was a musical play, **Tonight's the Night** by Frederick Thompson. Gladys Huddart was cast in the principal role of Victoria, the maid, and Fred Bell as Henry, '*the gay young bachelor*'. The other principals were: Gilbert James (playing an

Sally Cast Photo 1935

Back Row: *Jack Hefford, Charlie Nicholson, Leslie Wild, Bill Simon, Geoffrey Wilson, Jock Hetherington, Clarence Jeffries, Nelson Chicken, Eric Bewsher, Tony Millington, Ronnie Dallas* and *Tom Henderson.*
4th Row: *Lena Lewthwaite, Dorrie Faulder, Mary Mitchell, Ann Taylor, Kitty Bell* and *Kitty Dent.* 3rd Row: *Mary A.Wilson, Frank Williamson, Enid Fletcher, Freda Sharp, Mabel Sisson, Amy Tiffen, Annie Watson, Doreen Tiffen, Dorothy Birket, Rene Sisson, Ernest Wilkinson* and *Ivy Moorhouse.* 2nd Row: *Moyra Fletcher, Tom Ridley, Jos Beattie, Walter Deacon, Laura Harrison, Fred Bell, Margaret Mitchell, Gilbert James, Irene Rydiard, Leslie Williamson, Frank Entwhistle* and *Lizzie Wilson.* Front Row: *Norah Rydiard, Eleanor Little, Dorothy Mitchell* and *Norah Briggs.*

1935

In 1935 the WEA Players staged **Happy Journey to Trenton and Cambden** (with Elsie Ray, George Firn and Norah Banks) and **The Silver Box** (with Anthony Watson and Alma Clark). They also performed **Godstone Nunnery** and **Who Killed Me** around this time.

At the Grand Theatre, Tom Rawsthorn directed the musical, **Sally,** for the Operatic Society with Margaret Mitchell in the title role, playing opposite Fred Bell. In the show review in the local press, the reporter reflected on the economic depression of the 1930s and the Operatic Society's falling audiences.

1936

The final musical staged by the Operatic Society in the years immediately preceding the outbreak of World War II, was the April 1936 production of **Princess Charming** at the Grand Theatre. Irene Rydiard was cast in the leading role of Wanda the adventuress, with Walter Deacon in the comic role of Chuff. Betty Folder played the title role, Princess Charming, with Gilbert James as King Christian. This final show was directed by Tom Rawsthorn.

The WEA Players however, continued to stage plays in the town during this period and throughout the war. Their shows in the pre-war years included, **Love and How to Cure It**, **Women at War**, **Confutation of Wisdom**, and **Gap of the Winds**.

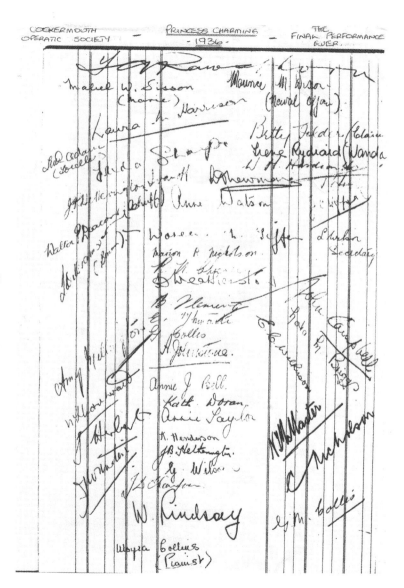

◁ Sentimental cast signatures from *'the final performance ever'* of Cockermouth Operatic Society

▷ Cast photo from the last musical performed by the Cockermouth Amateur Operatic Society in 1936, **Princess Charming**.. Seated on the left is the society's artistic director, *Tom Rawsthorn* and seated on the right of the photograph is founding member, *Lizzie Wilson*.

1936

1937

1938

1937

1938

In May 1937 the Operatic Society staged a variety show at the Grand Theatre, nostalgically billed - **Memories of the Opera - by past and present members.** Soloists in the concert included the founding musical director, Jonathan Huddart, Gladys Bell, Elsie Moscroft, Jim Huddart, Mary Oldroyd, Doreen Tiffen, Margaret Mitchell, Irene Rydiard, Gilbert James, Billy Byres, Harry Dixon and Walter Deacon.

The WEA Players staged the plays, **Herod**, **Mystery at Greenfingers** and **Boyd's Shop** around 1937.

The All Saints' Pantomime Company was formed in 1937 and in January 1938, staged their first Christmas show, **Babes in the Wood**, in the basement of Cockermouth Town Hall. The pantomime had a cast of thirty four which included William Gorley, Marion Nicholson, Ian Bowman, Maurice Cockton, T. Lister and Dorothy Wood.

The WEA Players performed **Pygmalion** at the Grand Theatre in December of that year with Edina Harris-Ward in the leading role, supported by John Pain, Alma Clark and George Firn. George made his début on the amateur stage in the early 1930s and appeared in many plays throughout the war years. He became a stalwart of the WEA Players, frequently taking leading roles throughout the1950s.

◁ The Grand Theatre in its hay-day in the 1930s

1939 to 1941

In the early 1940s the WEA Players began to stage their plays in Christ Church Rooms, behind the church itself in South Street. Opened as a Sunday school in 1884, the church rooms now became the 'home' of the Cockermouth Players and for the next thirty years they regularly entertained large audiences in the hall, staging two or three productions every year. Productions in the early war years included **Count Albany**, **Spring is in the Air**, **The Great Dark**, **Broken Fold**, **Unnatural Scene**, **Tobias and the Angel**, **End of the Beginning** and **Amazons on Broadway**.

Although the Operatic Society had disbanded before the outbreak of the Second World War, the Grand Theatre continued to provide live entertainment to Cockermouth's townsfolk, evacuees from the cities and servicemen home on leave. In May 1940, Red Howitzers' Concert Party performed there with a revue **The Old Kit Bag**, in aid of the local Hospital Supply Depot. Performers included Yvonne Ellis, Mollie Thorpe, Louie Kirkpatrick, Gerald Grice and Bob Wilson. The All Saints' Pantomime Company also continued to stage their annual pantomime in the Grand Theatre. In February 1941 they performed **Mother Goose** with a huge cast of sixty seven!

In December 1941 the WEA Players staged **If Four Walls** in Christ Church Rooms and in May of that year they produced the three-act comedy, **Nine Till Six**, by Phillip and Aimee Stewart. **Nine Till Six** had a large cast of fifteen, which included, Winnie Billington, Katie Burgess, Norah Banks, Betty Grimshaw, Mollie Yeomans, Helen Cooper, Margaret Hayton, Elsie Ray, Eileen Scott, Dorothy Chicken, Gwenyth Jones, Kathleen Sampson, Alma Clark, Nancy Birkett and Jean Briggs.

△ Christ Church Rooms behind the Church in South Street was the home of the Cockermouth Players for over thirty years

1939
1940
1941

1942 to 1943

Senior, former members of the Operatic Society revived the Cockermouth's Minstrel Group during World War II. Originally formed at the turn of the century, the 'Black & White Minstrels' provided very popular war time entertainment in the town, as can be judged from the following article which appeared in the local press:

'Minstrels are missed: Where are the versatile entertainers who smeared burnt coke on their faces, strummed banjos and clicked the 'Bones' as they sang plantation songs to large audiences in the town and district a few years ago? We refer of course to Cockermouth Christy Minstrels. As a combination they seem to have dispersed, which is a pity because they not only aided good causes but provided most acceptable shows.

A revival would be welcomed. Two of the originals, Messrs. F. Williamson and W. Slater, who were also principals, make a popular turn in solo and duet at minor concerts and dinner parties. Mr Slater's version of 'Black-eyed Susan' is still a winner, and the pair cut the same capers, crack the same jokes and sing the same songs as they did in the heyday of the Minstrels.'

In April 1943, the local press heralded the *Christy Minstrel Revival* when the Cockermouth Minstrel Group staged the first of three war time variety shows. Frank Williamson, who had first appeared in the 1927 Operatic Society's production of **Florodora,** was back on stage, as was the society's founding musical director, Jonathan Huddart, who acted as Interlocutor

for the show. The spectacular starred Stanley Kennon, Steve Hankin, Billy Slater and Joe Parker. Joining them on stage were: Messrs. S. Nash, Eric Bewsher, J.W. Bewsher, A. Bradley, A. Burton, Denis Clark, Ronnie Collins, James Cleeland, John Huddart, John Jeffries, J. Huddart, H.D. Kirkbride, G. Gorley, L. Miller, A. Millington, Tom Sealby, John Riley, Joe Slater, Bill Starkie, J. Tiffen, Bert Ferguson, Stanley Logan, J. Wood, Cliff Whitehead, J. McKernan, G. Thomas, H. Buglar, William Lindsay, R. Hindmoor, E. Wilkinson, H. Evans and J. Cartlidge. The company performed their variety show at Workington's Princess Hall in July 1943, where John Campbell was again the Musical Director. Jim Huddart, John Wood and Frank Entwistle joined the cast for the Workington show.

Along the road in South Street's Christ Church Rooms, the WEA Players were performing **Ladies in Retirement** and **Cradle Song** in 1943. The cast of **Cradle Song** included Norah Banks, Hilda Grave, Winifred Billington, Elsie Ray, Margaret Hayton, Alma Clark and George Firn.

▷ Cockermouth Christy Minstrels

sty Minstrel

and Variety Show

and Tuesday, 19th and 20th April, 1943

Commence 7-30 p.m.

ELS.—Messrs. S. Hankin, S. Ash, E. Bewsher, J. W.
Bewsher, A. Bradley, A. Burton, F. Clark, R.
Collins, J. Cleeland, J. Huddart, J. Jeffries, H.
D. Kirkbride, G. Gorley, L. Miller, A. Millington,
J. Parker, T. Sealby, J. Riley, J. Slater, W.
Slater, W. Starkie, J. Tiffen, R. Ferguson, S.
S. Kennon, J. McKernan, G. Thomas,
Buglar, W. Lindsay, R. Hindmoor, E. Wil
son, H. Evans, J Cartlidge, J. W. Huddart
OYS.—J. Wood, M. Cussons, M. Hoblin, A. Burns, J. Appl
K. Bowman, M. Denwood, S. Logan, H. S
J. Mason, E. Starkie, E. Dickson, D. Clar

INTERLOCUTOR.—J. W. Hankin.
BONES.—S. KENNON, S. HANKIN
TAMBOS.—W. SLATER, J. PARKER

ORCHESTRA:—
E. H. Shiers, E. W. Milli
Connolly, R. Collister, A. Goodwin, R.
Contra Bass.—R.
Clarinet—J. Coul
son. Drums—A. Wats
Collister, Junr.

IN CAMPB

THE GRAND THEATRE
COCKERMOUTH

Christy Minstrel

SHOW

Monday & Tuesday, 17th & 18th July, 1944

COMMENCE 7-30 P.M.

—J. Black, A. Bradley, R. Buglar, J. Byers, W. Byers,
Cartlidge, R. Collins, J. Cleeland, E. B
Chapman, E. W. Cockton, H. Evans, G.
Hill, J. Jeffrey, J. Johnston, G. Gorley, L.
sour, W. Lindsay, A. Marley, S. Kennon, S. Logan,
J. Slater, J. Slater, W. Starkie, J. Riley, T. Sealby,
Tiffen, J. Wood, C. Whitehead, G. Thomas, J
T. Burgess.

ott, T. Birkett,   A. Davidson, M. Denwood
S. Logan, J. Mason, H. Smith, B. Walker.

Interlocutor: F. W. Williamson.
Kennon,   Jones: R. B. Collins
Slater   Tambo: W. Starkie.

uthard.   J. T. Barnett, E. W. Millican, H. Pattin
R. H. Cowper,   R. Cowper, B. Connolly,
D. Skillen,   A. Watson.

noforte: Frank Mitchell
Director: John Campbell
and Lighting: Mr. W. Wharton
Manager: Mr. F. Stretch.

The GRAND THEATRE
COCKERMOUTH

Christy Minstrel
Show

Monday and Tuesday
17th & 18th Sept. 1945

Commence at 7-30 p.m.

FULL ORCHESTRA
(Orchestral Arrangements by Jack Coulthard)

DANCES
Arranged by Albert Wilson

MBY MALE VOICE QUARTET

DIRECTOR ...

FRANK
W.

1943

The Grand Theatre,
Cockermouth

CHRISTY MINSTREL
SHOW
(For Cottage Hospital)

Monday and Tuesday,
2nd and 3rd June, 1947.

Commence at 7-30

INTERLOCUTOR F. W. WILLIAMSON
BONES S. KENNON   SAMBO W. SLATER
JONES S. HANKIN   TAMBO W. STARKIE
ORCHESTRA A. Connolly, J. Barnett, J. Coulthard,
D. Skillen, E. Skillen, C. Lister,
E. Bell, R. Collister, G. Jones,
W. Cowper, J. Cowper, G. Steel.
(Orchestral Arrangements by Jack Coulthard)
PIANOFORTE FRANK MITCHELL
MUSICAL DIRECTOR W. G. BYERS
STAGE MANAGER & LIGHTING W. WHARTON

1944

In April 1944 the Players performed Oscar Wilde's best known satirical comedy, **The Importance of Being Earnest**. Anthony Watson directed the comedy in Christ Church Rooms and the West Cumberland Times said: *'the unquestioned star of this production was George Firn in the role of the foppish, genial Algernon Moncrieff; a new instance of his versatility. He and Alex Graham, as John Worthing, JP, formed the ideal comedy duo upon whose escapades the entertainment is built..'*
Other members of the cast of **The Importance of Being Earnest** were: John Pain, Kathleen Hewitson, Anthony Watson, Margaret Hayton, Eileen Stothard, Edna Armstrong, Winifred Fielden and John Waugh.

Frank Williamson took over as Interlocutor for the July 1944 **Minstrel and Variety Show**, again staged at the Grand Theatre. John Campbell, the former orchestra conductor for the Operatic Society, was the Musical Director for all these shows and John Black, who had leading roles in their 1921 production **Pirates of Penzance** and their 1922 staging of **Mikado,** joined the minstrel line-up.

The part of Bones was played by Stanley Kennon who delighted the audience with *'Silvery Moon'.* Jones was played by Ronnie Collins and Tambo by Bill Starkie. Billy Slater, in the role of Sambo, entertained with the war-time hit song, *Lilli Marlene.* The Minstrels in the 1944 show were: J. Black, A. Bradley, H. Buglar, J. Byers, W. Byres, J. Cartlidge,

△ Cockermouth Christy Minstrels

J. Cleeland, W.F. Chapman, E.M. Cockton, H. Evans, G. Gorley, W. Hill, J. Jeffries, J. Johnston, S. Logan Snr., W. Lindsay, A. Marley, J. Riley, T. Sealby, J. Slater, G. Thomas, J. Tiffen, J. Wood, C. Whitehead, F. Williamson and T. Burgess.

1945

In January 1945 the Cockermouth Players put on a double bill of two plays, **Tudor Thorns** by T.B. Morris and **Ten Days Before the Wedding** by Lindsey Barbee. Throughout the war years and into the 1950s, drama groups in neighbouring towns frequently performed their plays in each other's towns, and these two plays were performed at the Theatre Royal in Workington in 1945. Similarly, the Players performed **There's No Problem** at the Theatre Royal in1949 and **Juno and the Paycock** in 1953.

The 1945 cast of **Tudor Thorns** was Kay Weaver, Norah Banks, Mollie Yeomans, Eileen Stothard, Mary Hannah, Maud Lister, Gwen Jones, Edna Armstrong and Elsie Ray. The cast of **Ten Days Before the Wedding** was Winifred Fielden,

Mollie Yeomans, Kathleen Johnston, Enid Hawcroft, Joyce Gilbert, Norah Banks, Alma Clark, Hazel Allison, Kathleen Hewitson, Hilda Grave, Mary Hannah and Dorothy Nixon. **Tudor Thorns** was directed by Winifred Fielden and **Ten Days Before the Wedding** by Alec Graham.

These two plays were followed by a production of **Silver Cord**, and then in May 1945, Anthony Watson directed **Orange Blossom** by Philip Johnson. The play, featuring Edna Armstrong, Francis Hambling, Joyce Gilbert, Enid Hawcroft, Joan Waugh, Charles Davison and Maude Lister, was one of four one-act plays entered in the Cumberland Drama League competition held in the Lorton Street Schoolroom. The other plays were performed by the Workington Marsh Boys' Club, the

Isel Players and the Great Broughton Drama Group. **Orange Blossom** was placed first in the first heat with 84 marks. Competition judge, Mr Campbell Robson from Edinburgh said, '… *from the very first moment, this play had a feeling of confidence which the other plays lacked. …. Edna Armstrong could spit it out like a Bren Gun.'* The production was ultimately placed third in the county final in Upperby, Carlisle in June 1945.

Dangerous Corner by J B Priestley was also staged in 1945, along with **Her Affairs in Order**, **Gaslight** and **Double Demon**. **Dangerous Corner** was directed by Elsie Ray in Lorton Street Hall and the cast included Hilda Grave, Maude Lister, Edna Armstrong, Hazel Allison, Alec Graham, Francis Hambling and George Firn.

Billy Byres, a former tenor with Cockermouth Operatic Society, who first appeared in the 1923 production of **Patience**, was Musical Director for the September 1945 Minstrel and Variety Show at the Grand Theatre. The dances were arranged by Albert Wilson and billed in this show were: John Riley and Troupe, Bill Starkie, Albert Wilson and Girls, Master R. Huck, Mr W. Metcalfe and the Flimby Male Voice Choir, Steve Hankin, J. Wilkinson, James Cleeland, Jim Bradshaw, Stanley Kennon, W. Metcalfe, Frank Williamson and Billy Slater. The Christy Minstrels gave a final performance at the Grand Theatre in June 1947. The proceeds from all the minstrel shows were donated to the Cockermouth Cottage Hospital.

1946

In April 1944, the West Cumberland Times reviewing the Player's production of Oscar Wilde's **The Importance of Being Ernest**, had written, '*Cockermouth now has one of the most capable amateur drama groups the county has ever known. The company would be justified on future occasions in endeavouring to secure a more commodious theatre*'.

In the post-war years, the Grand Theatre was almost exclusively used for cinema. 'The Picture House', screened films seven nights a week and the only live amateur show there was the annual Christmas Pantomime staged by The All Saints' Pantomime Company. The last film was shown in the Grand Theatre in 1971. Thereafter, Bingo was played in the theatre's final years before closure in 1975. In 1979 the property was sold to Cockermouth vet, Jack Sedgewick with a restrictive covenant preventing the building being used in the future for any form of entertainment. In 1986 the Grand Theatre was converted by Roger and Stephen Hannah into a veterinary clinic occupying the foyer and box-office areas, and a lighting shop in the former auditorium.

Despite the loss of the Grand Theatre, the Cockermouth WEA Players continued to thrive in the town. Elsie Ray, who was in the original Betty Wilson's Minstrel Group in 1917, directed many of the WEA plays. After the closure of the WEA rooms in Cockermouth's Main Street, the Players rehearsed '*amongst the ladies' feathers, bonnets and hats*' in the room above Elsie Ray's millinery shop.

△ *Billy Wharton*, the former manager of the Public Hall, was now the manager of the Grand Theatre and remained in this position until the final closure of the theatre in 1975. *Billy* is on the right of the photo taken in 1959 outside the Grand Theatre with his staff: L-R: *Walter Standage* (ticket collector), *Mary Pooley* (circle ticket sales) and *Olive Farrow* (stall ticket sales).

The Players again entered the Cumberland Drama League competition in March 1946 at the Rawnsley Hall in Keswick. The plays chosen were **The Valiant** and **Everybody's Husband**. **The Valiant** had a cast of six, comprising of Nora Banks, Kay Weaver, Alma Clark, Edna Armstrong, Gwen Jones and Alec Graham. **Everybody's Husband** by G. Cannan, was placed third in county final at Waterton Hall in Carlisle. Elsie Ray produced both plays.

◁ This photo of Regent House in Main Street, Cockermouth was taken by Bernard Bradbury in 1968. It shows the location of the WEA first floor rooms next to Regent Hairdressers where the Players rehearsed before moving over the street to Elsie Ray's hat shop.

△ Elsie Ray's hat shop in Main Street was used by the Cockermouth Players for their rehearsals after the closure of the WEA Offices on the opposite side of the street. This photo, taken in 1938, shows *Freda Sharp* and *Edith Watson* outside the shop proudly displaying a silver cup won in a competition to mark the coronation of George VI. *Freda* appeared in many of the Operatic Society musicals in the 1930s.

1946

1947

Christ Church Rooms was now the permanent venue for all the Cockermouth Player's productions. The stage was assembled in front of the room partition doors which then formed a proscenium arch. The set flats were stored in nearby premises and then assembled and painted for each production. The shows in the church rooms were very popular in the post-war years and the Cockermouth Players frequently enjoyed full houses.

△ Christ Church Rooms looking north. Seats would be set out here to form the Player's auditorium.

In January 1947, Elsie Ray directed **I Have Five Daughters** in the church rooms. Adapted from Jane Austen's novel 'Pride and Prejudice', the cast included Mollie Yeomans, Norah Banks, Sylvia Scott, Joan Waugh, Edna Armstrong, Margaret Hayton, Kathleen Hewitson, Gwen Jones, Anthony Millington, Alan Muller, Alec Graham, Francis Hambling, Kay Weaver and Maude Lister. The plays **Dark Brown** and **Granite** were also staged in 1947.

△ Christ Church Rooms - looking south. The stage was assembled in front of the room partition doors which then formed a proscenium arch.

1947

△ Olive Richardson throws a slipper at Nelson Chicken in a scene from **At Mrs Beam's** 1948

1948

The Players staged **Great Day**, **Doll's House** and **At Mrs Beam's** in 1948. **Great Day** featured Elsie Ray as Mrs Mott and Dorothy Chicken as Vicky Calder. In Ibsen's **Doll's House**, George Firn played Torvald Helmer and Nora Banks played Nora Helmer.

The photo shows a scene from **At Mrs Beam's**, in which Olive Richardson is seen throwing a slipper at Nelson Chicken. Olive's daughter, Trisha, was a programme-seller in the early 1950s and recalled one occasion

in the middle of a thriller, when her mother had to place a candle in the window as a warning to an escaped prisoner. When she pulled back the curtain, there stood the stage manager, Joe Burnett, holding up the window frame!

1949

In 1949, a play written by one of the Cockermouth Players, Gwyneth Jones, and performed by the group, came second in the British Drama League competition in London. They staged Gwen's play, **There's No Problem** at the Scala Theatre at 58 Charlotte Street, off Tottenham Street in London's West End. Twenty years later the Scala Theatre was destroyed by fire. There had been a theatre on the site since 1772!

The Players' original cast at the Scala Theatre, directed by Gwen Jones, included Kathleen Clark, Anthony Watson, Joan Waugh, Ivor Newton, Winifred Collins and Elsie Ray. The play was subsequently staged in Cockermouth, Keswick, Carlisle, Abbeytown, Workington, Braithwaite, Dovenby and Brigham. Societies in Penrith and Ulverston

also produced Gwen's play. The cast of **There's No Problem** at the Theatre Royal in Workington were Marjorie Lee, Nelson Chicken, Alice Denholm, Betty Chicken, Jean Graham and Derek Barrett.

The Cockermouth Players celebrated their 21st Anniversary in October 1949 with excerpts from eight of their past productions. Their founder, Alida Lochead, travelled from Dorset to join the celebrations. Other members who came from afar included Molly Hodgson (the group's first secretary) who had travelled from Hereford, Lillian Jeffries from Iver in Buckinghamshire, and Tom Silvester from Derby. The Players' long-standing producers, Anthony Watson and Elsie Ray, narrated the evening's performances.

On their celebratory evening, Tom McAdam joined the members of the original cast to perform the extracts from **The Valiant** (1931 and 1937) and **The Whiteheaded Boy** (1934). He was joined by John Pain who played Father Daley in **The Valiant**. Bernand Conolly joined the original cast members, Elsie Ray and Molly Hodgson, in the extract from **The Tragedy of Man** (1931).

Hilda Banks supplemented some of the original cast in the extracts from **Orange Blossom** (1945) and **There's No Problem** (1949). Similarly, Ian Conolly and Joan Waugh joined some of the original cast for the extract from **Happy Journey** (1945) and Tom Graham stood in as Professor Higgins in the extracts performed from **Pygmalion** (1938). In these extracts Bernard

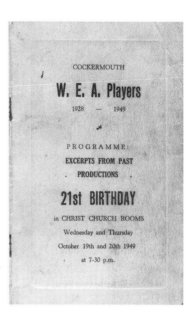

△ WEA Players 21st Birthday Programme 1949

Conolly (who was not in the original cast) played the part of Eliza's suitor, Freddy. In the extracts performed from the **Cradle Song** (1943), Olive Richardson and Celia Burgess joined others from the original cast.

1950

1951

1952

The Dear Departed, by Stanley Houghton, was performed in 1949 or 1950 by the Cockermouth Players. The one-act comedy had a cast of four men and three women. Around 1950-1951 the Players also staged **Pink String and Sealing Wax** and **Give Me Yesterday**.

In 1951, Anthony Watson directed Nelson Chicken, Norah Banks, Michael Denwood, Tom Graham, Margaret Todd, Bernard Conolly, Betty Chicken, Joe Wilkinson and Tom McAdam in **Outward Bound** by Sutton Vane. Around this time, the group also performed **The Paragon** and the John Dighton comedy, **The Happiest Days of Your Life**.

In October 1952, the Cockermouth Players staged **The Heiress** by Ruth and Augustus Goetz who had based their play on a novel by Henry James. The lengthy, two act play was staged for three nights in Christ Church Rooms and received great commendation in the local press. They described the play as '… *a long and exacting play for amateurs'* and applauded Elsie Ray's production as '… *a credit to all concerned and especially the producer … as one of the playgoers aptly remarked - it was just Miss Ray's "cup of tea".* The newspaper went on to report: '… *How thoroughly the locals captured the atmosphere of family life in Victorian times, and what feats of memorising they achieved! They have rarely been seen or heard to better advantage. The production was notable for the personal triumph in*

the name-part of Ruth Sims, a Great Clifton school teacher, who really excelled in her first major role on the local amateur stage.' Others making their first appearance in a full-length play were Betty Lett, who played the devoted family maid, and Ian Walker who played Arthur Townsend. Of them the newspaper said, ' …. *Both rose to the occasion admirably and Ian's make-up was a masterpiece.'* Other members of the cast included, Tom McAdam, Hilda Banks, Dorothy Chicken, Joan Jennings, Jim Burdekin and Kathleen Hewitson.

The Poltergeist was also performed by the Players around 1952 or 1953.

1950

1951

1952

1953

In 1953 the Cockermouth WEA Players were billed as simply the Cockermouth Players when they took their production of **Juno and the Paycock** to Workington. The production at the Theatre Royal was billed as a 'private performance' as public performances were restricted to only two or three each year under the terms of the Workington Playgoers Club lease of the premises from the Graves Cinema & Theatre Organisation. 'Private performances' were however open to Workington Playgoers Club members and the theatre was usually full!

The eighteen-strong cast, directed by Anthony Watson, starred George Firn as Captain Jack Boyle and Olive Richardson as his wife, June Boyle. Olive's daughter, Sheila, remembered the newspaper reporting that her mother had *'practised the accent as she did her housework'* but that George Firn who played 'Captain' Jack Boyle *'grew up in Cleator Moor where they spoke with Irish accents anyway'*! Other members of the cast of **Juno and the Paycock** were Leslie and Heather Kennaugh (Johnny & Mary Boyle) , Nelson Chicken (Joxer Daly), Kathleen Graham (Mrs Maisie Madigan), John Huddleston ('Needle' Nuggart, a Taylor), Elsie Ray (Mrs Tancred), Tom Graham (Jerry Devine), Jim Burdekin (Mr Bentham), Anthony Watson (An Irregular Mobilizer), Joe Wilkinson (Irregular), Ian Walker (Irregular and sewing machine man), Frances Hambling (a coal block vendor), Joe Burnett and Bob Wilson (furniture removal men), Josephine Gilbert and Maud Lister (two neighbours).

In a personal message to the Cockermouth Players, Sean O'Casey, the author of **Juno and the Paycock**, wrote, *'Juno and the Paycock was written many years ago, when strife ruled Ireland and men and women took a sadistic pleasure out of injury to, and the death of others. Now, after so many years it tires the mind to think of all its stupidity and although we haven't yet buried the gun, the conscience of man is more flexible towards stretching into a finer sense of brotherhood and co-operation. All that happened in this play, or almost all, happened in the house where I once lived, a tenement house still standing. Even the young man who was 'found dead on a lonely road in Finglass' lived there and was a friend of mine – I have his photograph here with me now. A terrible thing when romantic youth start shooting each other, all mad for a curious abstract idea of their native land. I hope the Cockermouth Players may enjoy themselves doing it, and I am fond enough of the play to hope that they may do it well. My best wishes to them.'*

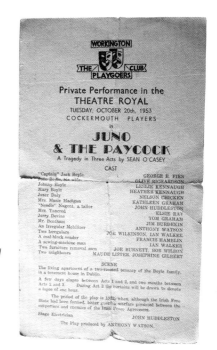

△ Cockermouth Players'
Juno & The Paycock
at the Theatre Royal in 1953

1954

Cockermouth's only live performance at the Grand Theatre in 1954 was the All Saints' Pantomime Company's **Goodie Two Shoes** '… *and what a lively performance it was'* reported the West Cumberland Times. Produced by the veteran director, Elizabeth Wilson and starring father- daughter combination, Joseph Marsh and his daughter Jean in the title role, the pantomime had a cast of over fifty and played to capacity audiences in March of that year. Geoff Reid and Bill Pooley provided a comically villainous two-some as Sir Thomas Gripes and Graball, his servant. Ann Taylor played the dame, Bill Gorley, the school inspector, George Carruthers, the farmer, and Joyce Maugham his wife. Winifred Roe was the Fairy Queen, Raymond McKay played

Tommy, and Muriel Staynton played Annette.

Others in the cast included: Edna Young, Pat Stephenson, Joan Rook, William Messenger, Audrey Huddart, Brenda Winter, Sally O'Neil (Villagers, Spanish ladies etc.), Carole Bell, Kay Flynn, Jean Hefford, Elizabeth Knight, June Moffat, Maureen Slack, Brenda Winter (Fairies etc.), Barbara Barton, Eleanor Burns, Barbara Cameron, Edna Cameron, Pamela Coulthard, Doreen Carruthers, Margaret Ellis, Jacqueline Hefford, Jennifer Huntington, Jennifer Logan (Seniors), Janice Canfield, Heater Crellin, Marie Davison, Brenda Kennon, Margeret Lister, Elizabeth Reid, Joan Stephenson, Nola Smith, Gwen Thompson,

Barbara Wedgwood, Margaret Wilson, Moira Winter (Juniors).

In the same month the Cockermouth Players won through to the final round of the one act play festival at Carlisle with the Elsie Ray production of **Ma Vatch** by T.V. Morris. Betty Lett played the title role supported by Tom Graham, Dorothy Bell, Pat Lothian and Bernard Conolly.

In April 1954 **Quiet Night**, by Dorothy Blewett, was performed by the Players on three consecutive nights in Christ Church Rooms. The three-act play set in the stark, colourless, service section of a ward in an Australian Hospital, was directed by Elsie Ray. The West Cumberland Times reported that '*the Cockermouth Players set

themselves a difficult exercise in personality-painting and carried it out triumphantly.'* The key figure in the play's web of over night drama was the character of Sister Frances Rankin played by Kathleen Hewitson. The reviewer said her performance was '*unfaltering through a long role'* and that she '*treated the troubles of her staff, the mental and physical distresses of her patients and her own emotional upheavals with subtle variations of the all-pervading cool detachment of the nurse.'* Playing the principal role of a patient (Mrs. Leila Clayton), Norah Ray, according to the West Cumberland Times, '*gave a convincing display of mounting hysteria on her frequent invasions of the service room.'* Dorothy Bell and David Brown, in the doctor-nurse liaison '*made a delightful team

Jim Dagnall at Cockermouth's Pantomime

which the audiences immediately took to heart.' Others in the cast were: Hilda Banks, Brenda Rogerson, Betty Chicken, Marjorie Lee, Heather Kennaugh, Constance Maughan, Bernard Conolly, Maude Lister and Leslie Kennaugh. The West Cumberland Times singled out Heather Kennaugh as the play's 'silver lining', without whom 'the play would have been infinitely poorer'.

▷ Jim Dagnall's cast cartoon in the West Cumberland Times on 6th March 1954

1954

1955

1956

The only record found of an amateur production in 1955, was the Cockermouth Players' staging of **Corinth House** in Christ Church Rooms on 13th, 14th and 15th April.

The Cockermouth Players produced two plays in 1956. Nora Ray and Hilda Banks jointly directed **School for Spinsters** followed, later in the year, by Hilda Banks's production of **Off The Deep End.** Rehearsals for **School for Spinsters** by Roland Pertwee, were held in the Papcastle home of George Firn of whom the newspaper review said, '...*acting honours go to George Firn as a stern, hypocritical Victorian father.*'

▷ **Off The Deep End** 1956.
L-R *Janet Smith, Maude Lister, Robert Wilson, Edna Sinclair* and *Marjorie Lee.*

School for Spinsters 1956 Pictured here are (left to right) *Betty Chicken, Olive Richardson* and *Edna Sinclair*.
The other four members of the cast of eight were: *Nelson Chicken, Jean Graham, David Brown* and *Barbara Goodfellow*.

1956

1957

1957

Elsie Ray died in 1957, after nearly thirty years associated with the Cockermouth Players as both a director and performer.

Hilda Banks was again the director in April 1957 for the Players' tense, psychological thriller, **Murder Mistaken**, written by Janet Green.

Edna Sinclair directed the Players' next production in October 1957, Kenneth Horne's comedy, **A Lady Mislaid**. The spinster sisters in the play, Jennifer and Ester Williams, were, according to the local newspaper, *'skilfully enacted by Betty Chicken and Jean Graham'*. It went on to report that *'…the comedy has wit and suspense, and the Players are at ease and hold attention throughout'*.

The play also featured Hilda Banks, Frank Stonehouse, Nelson Chicken, Joe Wilkinson and Mollie Hayton.

△ **Murder Mistaken** 1957. The photo shows four of the six characters in the play. Left to right they are: *Dorothy Chicken, Jeffrey Dye, Edna Sinclair* and *Joe Wilkinson*. Also appearing in **Murder Mistaken** were *Barbara Goodfellow* and *Kathleen Hewitson*.

1958

The Players chose the comedy **Quiet Weekend** for their Spring production in 1958. Written by Ester McCracken in 1946, the three-act play had a thirteen-strong cast comprising of: Joe Wilkinson, Kathleen Jones, Barbara Goodfellow, Nancy Wood, Kathleen Hewitson, Nelson Chicken, Anne Wilkinson, Joan Jennings, Jeffrey Dye, David Brown, Edna Sinclair, Robert Hewitt and Janet Smith. Hilda Banks was again the play's director.

Edna Sinclair and Maude Lister teamed up in October to produce **No Escape**. Two young newcomers, Alice Denholm and Derek Barrett, *'acted in surprisingly accomplished style'* – according to the local newspaper. George Firn made a welcome return to the stage, joining the other cast members, Jean Graham and Marjorie Lee.

△ **No Escape** 1958 L-R *Alice Denholm, Nelson Chicken* and *Betty Chicken*

1959

In 1955 the comedy **Sailor Beware** opened in the West End, with Peggy Mount in the leading role of the ultimate battleaxe, Emma Hornett. The film version in 1956, co-starring Gordon Jackson and Thora Hird, catapulted Peggy Mount to stardom.

In 1959, the Cockermouth Players staged their own production of **Sailor Beware** directed, for the first time, by Jean Graham. Edna Sinclair played the Peggy Mount character of which the local newspaper said, '*Emma Hornett – at the hands of Edna Sinclair … what a harping, carping, nattering creature she became, with human emotions, polished lino and sideboard tops all mixed up in her scale of values.*' Playing opposite her was Joe Wilkinson in the role of her hen-pecked husband, Henry.

John Millington, according to the press '*…made a great first time hit, assuming the Scots accent to perfection as Carnoustie Bligh A.B.*' and Derek Barrett '*ably portrayed*' his side-kick, Albert Tufnell A.B. Michael Crawford played the aptly named Reverend Oliver Purefoy.

▷ A scene from the Players' 1959 production of **Sailor Beware** – a tea-cup reading session suggests that the bridegroom will fail to turn up.

L-R: *Edna Sinclair* (Emma Hornett), *Joan Jennings* (playing Edie Hornett, the lack-lustre spinster sister jilted at the altar), *Mollie Hayton* (the nosey neighbour), *Sarah Jarvis* (the inaptly-named Daphne Pink) and *Dorothy Bell* (as the betrothed bride-'mother's little girl').

1959

1960

In February 1960, three one act plays were performed by the Cockermouth Players at the newly opened 'Derwent Cultural and Education Centre' on Castlegate Drive. The plays, **Sunday Costs Five Pesos** by Josephine Niggli, **Continental Customs** by Leonard de Frannequen and **Riches and Rags** by Colin Cooper were sponsored by the Inner Wheel Club and about £40 was raised for the World Refugee Year fund.

Zoe Dawson directed the one act Mexican comedy, **Sunday Costs Five Pesos**, starring Alice Marley, Joan Jennings, Michael Crawford, Ann Wilkinson and Sally Benson. Commenting on the fight scene staged by Alice Marley and Joan Jennings, the local newspaper reported, '…. *rarely has such action*

1960

△ Derwent School on Castlegate Drive, opened in 1958

been seen on the stage locally, all wondering at the spirit of the contestants, whose exchanges were the very opposite of the namby-pamby passes often seen when this play is given by amateurs. It was well that the performance was for one night only. Even so, the two young ladies involved will probably be nursing their bruises for a week'.

From Mexico to Europe, Gwen Jones directed an all-female cast in **Continental Customs**, a one act comedy set in a customs house. The play featured Janet Smith as a dancing teacher, Hilda Banks as a lady seeing life, Kathleen Hewitson as a business woman, Georgina Gill as a honeymooner, Dorothy Bell a woman of the world and Betty Chicken as a hostess.

The third play, **Riches and Rags**, was directed by Leonard Green and told the story of two old codgers (played by Bob Tinker and Joe Wilkinson) who win on a football pools coupon. The play also featured Olive Richardson, Dorothy Chicken, John Millington and Jean Graham.

In May 1960, Gwen Jones and Hilda Banks staged the domestic drama **Symphonie Pastorale** by Millicent George at the Derwent Centre and subsequently entered their production in the Cumberland Drama League's three-act play festival. The cast of six was led by Leonard Green who was described as *faultless as the pastor* in the local newspaper. Dorothy Bell played Claire, the blind girl. Also appearing were Jean Graham, Michael Crawford, Sally Benson and John Millington.

The Players returned to Christ Church Rooms in October 1960 to perform a three-act play, **Ladies in Retirement** by Edward Percy and Reginald Denham. The group were now based behind Walter Clark's Dress Shop in New Street.

The costumes, props etc., were stored in a garage and rehearsals took place in rooms above. Cockermouth Library, where Player's member, Dorothy Bell worked, was also used for rehearsals, as was space across the river in Miller's Factory. Later the group rehearsed in the new Derwent School where drama was linked into further education programmes.

The early 1960s appear to have been a barren time for theatre in Cockermouth with no shows reported in the local newspapers. However Gwen Jones and Hilda Banks, together with Players' stalwarts, Joe Wilkinson, Dorothy Bell and Jean Graham continued acting or producing plays throughout the 1960s and well into the 1970s.

1960

△ *Bob Tinker* and *Joe Wilkinson* (in night caps) with *John Millington* and *Olive Richardson* (playing the lady from the 'Pools' presenting a cheque) in **Riches and Rags** 1960.

1965

Summer pantomimes became a regular feature on the Cockermouth calendar in the mid 1960s. Sadie Grave (now Sadie Cussons), who had choreographed and starred in many of the Operatic Society shows at the Grand Theatre in the 1920s and 1930s, ran a successful dance school in Cockermouth. Drawing on experienced local actors and singers, the summer pantomimes at the Derwent Centre on Castlegate Drive became a popular annual product of her dance school.

△ Rehearsals for Sadie Cussons' Dance School production of **Cinderella** 1965.
Sadie Cussons, holding the music score, is standing by the piano on the left of the picture.
Others in the picture are: Back Row L-R: *Joan Sharp, Elizabeth Scott, Michael Sumpton, Raymond Sumpton* and *George Carruthers.* Middle Row (standing) L-R: *Harold Smith, Sadie Cussons, Laura Todd, Geoff Reid, Chris Todd, Billy Pooley, Joyce Maugham, Dererk Barrett, Kathleen Todhunter, Elaine Hilton* and *Susan Lindsay.* Middle Row (seated): *Jack Coulthard* (holding violin) and *June Perkins* (on the piano stool). Front Row (seated) L-R: *Anne Lindsay, Margaret Reid, Janet Shand* and *Dorothy Reid.*

1966

In June 1965 Sadie Cussons produced and directed **Cinderella** with Kathleen Todhunter in the title role and Joyce Maugham as the principal boy, Price Charming. Derek Barrett and Chris Todd played the ugly sisters, George Carruthers and Bill Pooley (Spif and Cop, the broker's men), Harold Smith and Geoff Reid (the Baron and Baroness), and Elaine Hilton played Buttons. Other principals were Laura Todd as Dandini; Chris Barr as the Watchman; Frank Cussons as the Sergeant; Susan Lindsay, the Fairy Godmother and Michael and Raymond Sumpton as the heralds.

The West Cumberland Times said: *'The show is staged without scenery, but the brilliant costumes provide the necessary colour for a production of this kind, and the most spectacular scene of all is when Cinderella is taken off to the ball in a golden coach sprinkled with coloured lights and drawn by a large band of tiny fairies. Cockermouth is not short of people to play the comedy roles, and George Carruthers and Bill Pooley win most of the laughs as Spif and Cop, the broker's men, filling in with a highly original magicians' act, and Derek Barrett and Chris Todd are at their funny best as the ugly sisters....... Mrs Cussons had done a grand job in producing* **Cinderella** *and in training the dancers for over a score of intricate routines.'*

Joe Wilkinson, a former Chairman of the Cockermouth Players, directed **Watch It Sailor** at the Derwent Centre in April 1966. Now billed as the Cockermouth Drama Group, (although still referred to in the local press as *'the Players'*) their cast, in this sequel to **Sailor Beware**, starred Joan Jennings in the leading role of Emma Horrett, with Bob Tinker playing her hen-pecked husband, Henry. Bob subsequently resurrected the role of Henry Horrett in 1975 in yet another sequel by Philip King and Falkland Cary, **Rock-a-bye Sailor**. He became a leading figure in the Cockermouth Drama Group, appearing every year in leading roles in the Players' productions throughout the next decade.

Ann Howitt played the bride-to-be, Shirley Hornett, in **Watch It Sailor**. Colin Gibson and George Pattinson played the courting sailors, Carnoustie Bligh A.B. and Albert Tufnell A.B. Doug Pattinson played Lieutenant Commander Hardcastle R.N, Dinah Thompson (Mrs. Lack, the nosy neighbour), Jean Graham (Edie Hornett, the lack-lustre spinster sister jilted at the altar), and Doreen Wilson (Daphne Pink).

In June 1966, Sadie Cussons staged another 'summer pantomime', **Dick Whittington**, with Barbara Goodfellow in the title role, Joyce Maugham as Alice and Elizabeth Scott as their faithful cat. Profits from the pantomime were donated to the Cockermouth Congregational Church funds.

1966

△ **Watch It Sailor** 1966 cast photo.
L-R standing: *Bob Tinker, Joan Jennings,
Doug Pattinson, Dinah Thompson,
Colin Gibson, Jean Graham.*
Seated: *George Pattinson, Ann Howitt*
and *Doreen Wilson.*

△ **Something to Hide** 1967 cast photo.
L-R: *Diana James, Jean Graham, Bob Tinker,
Colin Gibson, Roger Anning, Elisabeth
Millican* and, seated, *June Ashworth.*

1967

1968

Joe Wilkinson directed the thriller, **Something to Hide**, by Leslie Sands in April 1967, again at the Derwent Secondary School. The cast were: Diana James (Stella), Jean Graham (Miss Cunningham), Bob Tinker (Mr Purdie), Colin Gibson (Inspector Davies), Roger Anning (Howard Holt), Elisabeth Millican (Julie) and June Ashworth (Karen Holt).

In May 1968, Joe Wilkinson again directed the drama group's Spring production at the Derwent Centre. **Spring And The Oakleys,** a comedy by Wilfred Massey and Rosemary West, featured Colin Gibson (Harry Oakley), Joan Jennings (Mrs MacGregor), Rhoda Ritchie (Karen Oakley), Bob Tinker (Adam Wardale), Nelson Chicken (Steven Oakley), Ann Howitt (Kim Oakley), Doreen Wilson (Wendy Travis), June Ashworth (Heather Wardale) and Chris Dunnobin (Sandy Brennan).

△ Cockermouth School hall 1958
The school hall on Castlegate Drive used by the Drama Group for their productions throughout the 1960s (and later by CADS in the 1980s).

1970

1972

The Cockermouth Players were again largely dormant in the late 1960s and early 1970s. There was an exception in 1970 when a professional actress, Phillipa Read from Braithwaite, formed a group called 'Experiments in Entertainment' based at the Derwent Centre. Cockermouth Players' veteran, Hilda Banks, joined the group, who presented a double bill at the Centre in the May of that year. The first of the two plays, **The House of Bernarda Alba** by Federico Garcia Lorca, featured projected images of a Spanish funeral procession accompanied by the recorded tolling of Crosthwaite Church bell at Keswick and by live guitar music from Keswick's Robin Dawson. In the second play, **The Happy Journey**, Hilda Banks was joined by Gilbert Johnstone, Paul

Basnett and Gillian Ogden (all of Cockermouth).

This though appears to have been the only production staged by 'Experiments in Entertainment' and the curtains remained closed on the stages in Cockermouth until 1972.

All Saints' Church Rooms on Kirkgate

In May 1972, the Times & Star newspaper headline 'Players left audience asking for more' welcomed the return of the Drama Group. The review of the two plays started with: 'The hibernating talents of the Cockermouth Amateur Dramatic Society revived this week with the presentation of a double bill in the All Saints' Rooms in connection with

the Cockermouth Festival. The two plays were well received, so well that playgoers left asking why the Society doesn't do more.'

The revival was thanks to Hugh Turner who produced the two plays under the title, **Oh Thespians**. The revived group was billed as the 'Cockermouth Amateur Dramatic

1970

1972

Society' and a new venue, All Saints'
Church Rooms on Kirkgate, was found.
Built in 1896 on the site of the old
Grammar School, All Saints' Church
Rooms had a seating capacity of 300
in its large first-floor hall and became
the 'home' of the drama group for the
next decade.

The first of the two plays, **A Privy
Council** by W.P. Drury and Richard
Pryce, was based on a fictitious
incident in the life of Samuel Pepys.
Colin Gibson starred in the title role
with Diana James (Mrs Pepys), Bob
Tinker, Hugh Turner, June Ashworth,
Florence Pearl and Rhoda Ritchie.

The second play on the bill, **Its
Autumn Now** by Philip Johnson, was
set in 1900 and featured Hugh Turner,
Dorothy Bell, Florence Pearl, Bob Tinker,
Rhoda Ritchie, and Diana James.

1972

△ **A Privy Council** 1972 L-R *Diana James* (Mrs Pepys), *Colin Gibson*
(Samuel Pepys), *Rhoda Ritchie, June Ashworth* and *Bob Tinker*.

1973

1973

In the Spring of 1973, Ernest Pearl took the reins of the drama society, and their name reverted to the Cockermouth Drama Group. Together with his wife Florence and secretary Bob Tinker, Ernie Pearl became the driving force behind the group for the next four years.

In March 1973, assisted by Joe Wilkinson and Nancy Gibson, Ernie produced three one-act plays in All Saints' Church Rooms.

Home is the Hunted featured Diana James, Rhoda Ritchie, Dorothy Bell, Florence Pearl, Bob Tinker and Colin Gibson. The cast performing **The Witching Hour** were: Jean Graham, Dorothy Bell, Rhoda Ritchie, June Ashworth,

1974

◁ 1973 Three one-act Plays: **Home is the Hunted, The Witching Hour** and **Green For Danger** L-R the actors are: *Florence Pearl, Dorothy Bell, Rhoda Ritchie* (seated), *Diana James, Jean Graham, Hilda Banks, June Ashworth, Bob Tinker* (seated) and *Colin Gibson.*

Diana James and Hilda Banks. Then Florence Pearl, Jean Graham, June Ashworth, Bob Tinker and Colin Gibson returned to the stage for the third play, **Green For Danger**.

The drama group's activities in Cockermouth remained linked to the Adult Education Drama Classes at the Derwent School and in 1974 the group staged three more one-act plays: **Without Portfolio, White Blackmail** and **World Without Men**. The classes were, however, very short of male actors, and in an article in the local newspaper in February 1974, the reporter wrote:

'.… *The Players number only two men among their acting strength, which not only makes heavy demands on their versatility but also restricts the repertoire of the company. It's more than a coincidence that one of the three act plays which they are to stage next week in All Saints' Church Rooms is* '**World Without Men**,' *which calls for an all female cast of seven,*

and another, '**White Blackmail**' *also features seven ladies and no men. Veterans Bob Tinker and Colin Gibson are outnumbered two to one in the third play* '**Without Portfolio**'.

White Blackmail did, however, introduce three newcomers, albeit females. Vivian Hodgson, Lola Foster and Pauline Peters joined the cast of this play, which featured veterans Hilda Banks, Dorothy Bell, Florence Pearl and Jean Graham.

The cast of **World Without Men** were: Hilda Banks, Diana James, June Ashworth, Jean Graham, Dorothy Bell, Rhoda Ritchie and Vivian Hodgson. **Without Portfolio** featured Hilda Banks, Pauline Peters, Diana James, Colin Gibson, June Ashworth and Bob Tinker.

In November 1974 Ernie Pearl produced **Fool's Paradise** by Peter Coke, with Jean Graham, Rhoda Ritchie, Peter Hodgson, Vivian Hodgson, Bob Tinker, June Ashworth, Diana James and Florence Pearl.

1973

1974

1975

Barbara Polkinghorne revived the pantomime tradition in January 1975 and assembled a large community cast to stage **Snow White and the Seven Dwarfs** at the Derwent School. Starring Alan Casine, Mike Hall, Trudi Malone, Dave Eadington, Marie Hoban, Derek Dearne and Erica Ashmore, all proceeds from the pantomime were used to help fund a swimming pool at the site of the former Drill Hall on Castlegate Drive.

However, the lack of male actors in the Cockermouth Drama Group continued to present problems for the society in 1975. In the programme for their Spring production of **The Danger Line**, Director/Producer Ernie Pearl wrote: *'If there is any particular play you would like us to perform please let us know and, providing the cast contains no more than three men, we shall be pleased to consider it amongst our future plans'!*

In November 1975 the Drama Group staged **Rock-a-bye Sailor,** another sequel to **Sailor Beware** by Philip King and Falkland Cary. Rhoda Ritchie this time played the role of Emma Hornett made famous by Peggy Mount. Bob Tinker again played her husband, Henry Hornett with Jean Graham (Eddie Hornett), Dorothy Bell (Mrs Florrie Lack), Michael Rooney (Albert Tufnell), Vivian Hodgson (Shirley Tufnell), Lola Foster (Daphne Bligh) and Peter Hodgson (Carnoustie Bligh). Still short of male actors, the character of Robert Stebbington was ingeniously adapted as a female part re-named 'Roberta Stebbington'

and played by June Ashworth. The show was directed by Hilda Banks.

▷ The cast of **The Danger Line** 1975. Left to right seated are: *June Ashworth and Dorothy Bell. Standing are: Bob Tinker, Hilda Banks, Peter Hodgson, Lola Foster, Michael Rooney,* and *Pauline Peters.*

1975

1976 marker: 1976

1976

There was an all-female cast of eight for the Players' **Motive for Murder** by Sam Bate in April 1976. Performed in All Saints' Church Rooms and directed by Ernie Pearl, the cast comprised of Florence Pearl, Rhoda Ritchie, Vivian Hodgson, Jean Graham, June Ashworth, Pauline Peters and Lola Foster.

In May, the Drama Group resurrected their production of **Rock-a-bye Sailor** and performed it on the stage of Keswick's famous Blue Box Century Theatre. This originally travelling theatre was built in 1952 and launched the careers of future stars such as Bob Hoskins, Helen Mirren and Tom Courtenay. The 'Blue Box' became a regular

◁ *Rhoda Ritchie* and *Moira Rees* in a scene from Cockermouth Drama Group's **Motive for Murder** 1976

summer visitor to Keswick from 1961 and, after more than two decades of touring, become a permanent Keswick resident in 1976. It remained in constant use until 1999 when it was finally replaced by the Lottery funded, £6.2m 'Theatre by the Lake'.

Fifteen years after the Drama Group's production of **Rock-a-bye Sailor**, Cockermouth's next drama group, CADS, also performed on the stage of the 'Blue Box' in 1991. They returned there again in 1992 and then, after another interval, performed on the studio stage of the new 'Theatre by the Lake' in 1999 and in every year thereafter from 2002 to 2005.

▷ Century Theatre's 'Blue Box Theatre' photographed in Keswick in 1991.

△ Cast of **Motive for Murder** 1976 Left to right *Florence Pearl, Rhoda Ritchie, Vivian Hodgson, Jean Graham, June Ashworth* (seated), *Moira Rees, Pauline Peters* and *Lola Foster*

1976

1977

1981

1977

1981

Around this time Ernie and Florence Pearl moved away from Cockermouth and the Drama Group, now with only three men and six women members remaining, was once again in sad decline.

In March 1977, Hilda Banks's final production, **Strike Happy**, was performed in All Saints' Church Rooms. The farcical comedy by Duncan Greenwood featured Dorothy Bell, Lola Foster, Peter Hodgson, Mike Rooney, Bob Tinker, Rhoda Ritchie, Vivian Hodgson and Lynn Hodgson. Mike Rooney had the leading role in **Strike Happy**, playing opposite Lola Foster. Mike recalled Lola's son in the audience objecting to his 'stage kissing', shouting out *'you can't kiss my mum'.*

The only production staged in Cockermouth from 1978 to 1980 is believed to be a touring, professional drama, **Ring of Hands.** This play, presented by 'Theatre Roundabout' in Christ Church Rooms in May 1979, featured Sylvia Read and William Fry.

Then in May 1981 Hugh Turner returned from Workington Playgoers' Club to once again try and revive the Cockermouth Drama Group. The play he directed in All Saints' Church Rooms was **Duet of Two Hands** by Mary Hayley Bell. Lola Foster had the leading role in the four hand play with Peter Hodgson, Dorothy Bell and John Taylor. **Duet of Two Hands** is however believed to be the final production of 'The Players'.

△ *Hugh Turner*

1984

In 1984, Bob Pritchard, a young English teacher working at Whitehaven School, placed an advert in several shop windows in Cockermouth canvassing interest in forming a new drama group.

Tucked away in High Sands Lane, the former 18th Century Wesleyan chapel where John Wesley was reputed to have preached, had recently been renovated by Cockermouth Town Council. On 10th September 1984 in the tiny converted Victoria Hall, a new drama group held its inaugural meeting. Approximately thirty people attended the meeting including Barbara Colley (who was later the driving force behind the opening of the Kirkgate Arts Centre), Chris and Dominic Constable, Mary Coote, Jan Dockwray, Eleanor Elliot, Chris George, Emma Gowan, Liz Harris, Phil King, John Perry, Bob and Liz Pritchard, Barbara Rothwell, Nick Stanley, Alison and Audrey Tozer, Len Wainwright, and Bob Tinker, the sole remaining member of the Cockermouth Players. From this meeting, the Cockermouth Amateur Dramatic Society was formed – known as CADS.

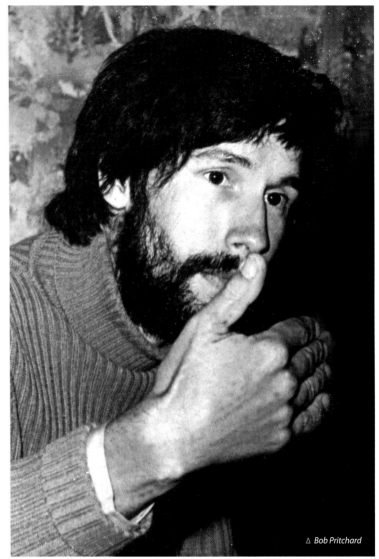

△ Bob Pritchard

1984

CADS first production on 14th and 15th December 1984 was a sketch show in the Victoria Hall. The balcony seating area was used as dressing rooms, reducing the ground floor seating capacity to less than thirty! This first production, **Christmas Crackers**, included **Christmas in the Trenches** (a sketch from **O What a Lovely War**); **Trouble At T'Mill** (Harold Pinter sketch, performed by Nick Stanley and Len Wainwright); **Infants' Nativity** (Grenfell monologue performed by Emma Cowan); **Dear Me** (self-penned sketch from John Perry); **Holly Bears A Berry** and a **Shepherds' Play** (which featured Bob Pritchard, Chris George, Judith Denwood, Stephen Coad and Pauline Benson).

△ *Bob Pritchard, Chris George* and *Len Wainwright in* **Christmas Crackers** 1984

1985

For the next decade, CADS led an almost Bedouin-like existence, rehearsing and performing wherever they could. Cockermouth School rooms were initially hired for rehearsal space before CADS found a base in the upper room of 'The Sportsman' at the foot of Kirkgate (converted in the mid 1990s, after standing derelict for a number of years, into a successful pub and micro-brewery, the 'Bitter End'). Meetings, and other social events, were held across the road in the 'Over The Top' café. Scenery and props were stored in an outbuilding in St.Helen's Street. Costumes were stored above Billy Bowman's overspill music premises in the Market Place. Lighting, sound equipment, wigs and make up were stored in the loft space of any willing member's home!

The Beauty of Buttermere (or **A Maiden Betrayed**) was chosen for CADS' first full-scale production. The play, based on the true story of Mary Robinson, was written in the 1970s by a former Workington Grammar School English teacher, Alasdair Brown and later was the subject of a successful novel by Melvyn Bragg entitled 'The Maid of Buttermere'. Melvyn Bragg's 1987 novel was adapted for the stage and had its world première in Keswick in 2009. CADS' musical comedy melodrama preceded this stage adaptation by 24 years.

▷ *Phil King* and *Pauline Benson* in
The Beauty of Buttermere 1985

1985

The Beauty of Buttermere was staged at Cockermouth School in April 1985. Pauline Benson, in the title role, headed a cast of approximately twenty actors which included Phil King, Jim Askew, Derek Dearne, Nick Stanley, Len Wainwright and Chris George. Phil Carswell, Cumbria Education's advisor for music, composed an original score for the drama. Bob Pritchard produced and directed the show, as well as taking part.

The group's next venture was the staging of the play-let **Pyramus and Thisbe** (from Shakespeare's **A Midsummer Night's Dream**) in the grounds of Cockermouth Castle.

◁ *Len Wainwright, Chris George* and *Bob Pritchard* in **Pyramus and Thisbe** from **A Midsummer Night's Dream** 1985

On a rain-soaked Saturday in September, a small, but brave crowd huddled under their umbrellas to witness the performances of Chris George, Bob Pritchard, Len Wainwright and others.

CADS performed their next full-scale production, **The Servant of Two Masters**, on the stage in the former Grammar School on Lorton Road. Directed by Chris George, the cast of twelve included Nick Stanley, Liz Harris, Emma Gowan, Des Mason and Bob Pritchard. The show was performed for two nights in Cockermouth, one night in the Cleator Moor Civic Hall and a final night at the John Peel Theatre in Wigton.

CADS returned to the Victoria Hall in December 1985 with another review, **Christmas Crackers II**.

1986

CADS' 1986 season opened in April with **Mixed Doubles**, a series of short plays by Alan Ayckbourn, Fay Weldon and Harold Pinter, linked with George Melly monologues. An eighteen strong cast included Marion Hughes, Nick Stanley, Fiona Day, Rachel Wallbank, Dominic Constable, Joanna Pritchard, Mair Collins, Laurie Mansfield, Jim Askew, Eleanor Elliott, Audrey Tozer and Chris George. The show was staged at the Lorton Road School and was produced by Bob Pritchard and Chris George.

In September 1986, Chris George produced a **Victorian Evening** of sketches in the Victoria Hall, and in December, CADS performed a Victorian melodrama, **Drunkard's Dilemma**, at Keswick School.

Also in December of that year, Bob Pritchard directed an eighteen-strong cast at Cockermouth School in the children's fantasy, **The Incredible Vanishing ....** Bob then broke new ground for CADS by staging this production at the Rosehill Theatre near Whitehaven. Built by Sir Miki Sekers in 1959, Rosehill once required audiences attending its prestigious shows to wear formal dress! Many leading artists performed at the Rosehill Theatre in the 1960s, including Yehudi Menuhin, John Gielgud, Judi Dench, Joyce Grenfell and Benjamin Britten. CADS were now following in some illustrious footsteps!

△ A scene from **The Incredible Vanishing....** in 1986, featuring *Laurie Mansfield* as PC Parker with *Barbara Rothwell* as Lulu Maguire and *Mary Coote* as Jenny Jones.

△ The cast of the September 1987 production of **Abigail's Party**
L-R *Edwina Brame, Len Wainwright, Liz Fitton, Alan Saunders* and *Margaret Fox.*

1987

CADS staged Mike Leigh's **Abigail's Party** twice in 1987. In February, the five strong cast of Liz Fitton, Len Wainwright, Margaret Fox, Des Mason and Carol Jamieson, collectively directed the comedy in the Victoria Hall. Then in September, the play was resurrected by Greg Greenhalgh, making his directorial début. For this second production, Alan Saunders replaced Des Mason and Edwina Brame took on the role of Susan played by Carol Jamieson in the earlier production. This new production was the first 'sold out' show for CADS. The only complaint from the local newspaper was that *'the lack of a stage resulted in a few stiff necks at the back of the auditorium.'* Cockermouth Town Council responded by funding the construction of some

△ **Hobson's Choice** 1987
L-R: *Beryl Balance, Edwina Brame, Steve Coad, Greg Greenhalgh, Mike Palmer* and *Mary Coote*

portable staging for use in future productions.

Cockermouth Grammar School combined with Derwent School in 1984 and closed its Lorton Road site in 1988. Before it closed,

CADS staged three productions there in 1987. The first of these, Harold Brighouse's classic comedy **Hobson's Choice**, was produced and directed by Chris George in the Spring. **Hobson's Choice** played to full houses on three consecutive

nights, with Greg Greenhalgh in the title role, Mary Coote playing his rebellious daughter, Maggie, and Mike Palmer in the role of the shoe-maker and reluctant suitor, Will Mossop.

Then in the summer of 1987, Bob Pritchard directed the CADettes (a youth wing of the society) at the former Grammar School in two, one-act plays. These plays were followed by another Victorian melodrama, **Ah Cruel Fate**, in the Victoria Hall, before the group toured in October with Willy Russell's **Educating Rita**. Greg Greenhalgh produced and Laurie Mansfield directed the two-hand comedy, with Beryl Balance in the title role and Chris George playing her university professor. With such a volume of lines to learn, Beryl wrote to Julie Walters, who had starred with Michael Caine in the successful film version of the play. In a hand-written reply, Julie Walters told Beryl *'if you work on the character's motivation in each scene, the lines will take care of themselves.'*

1987

CADS performance of **Educating Rita** at the former Grammar School was their final production there. For the second time however, CADS took their production on to Whitehaven to perform it for one night only at the Rosehill Theatre.

CADS 1987 season was rounded off with another children's fantasy, **The Heartless Princess**, performed by a cast of eleven at Cockermouth School. Peter Fox directed and Chris George produced the show starring Jayne Bendall as Prince Alexis and Ron Eaton as 'the Fox'.

◁ *Chris George* and *Beryl Balance* in **Educating Rita** 1987

▷ *Ron Eaton* as 'the Fox' in **The Heartless Princess** 1987

1987

1988

In February 1988, Greg Greenhalgh produced and directed the fast-moving political comedy **Can't Pay, Won't Pay**, written by the Italian satirist and Nobel Prize-winner, Dario Fo. This five-hander 'riot of a play' played to capacity audiences in Cockermouth's Victoria Hall and Whitehaven's Rosehill Theatre.

In April, Bob and Liz Pritchard staged **The Crucible**, in the unique atmosphere of the eighteenth century Quaker Meeting House in the village of Pardshaw. Bob designed a promenade performance of Arthur Miller's powerful drama, which the Times and Star newspaper described as 'an unforgettable experience …. created in a spellbinding atmosphere.'

The twenty-five strong cast featured

Marion Hughes, Mike Palmer, Keith Irving, Mary Coote and Chris George in the principal roles. CADS production of **The Crucible** scooped the 1988 Cumbria Drama Award in the category of best stage play.

Still on the search to find a suitable performing venue in Cockermouth, CADS staged a cabaret evening, **Friday Night Live**, in 'The Office' night club in South Street in June 1988. Then producer Chris George found a venue which was to become CADS 'home' for the next seven years. The new owner of the Globe Hotel in Cockermouth was a keen thespian and obtained a performance licence to stage theatre once again in the hotel's ballroom. Scenery, staging, lighting equipment and props all had to be man-handled up the fire-escape

ladder from the basement of the hotel, but undeterred, CADS staged their first play, **Ten Times Table**, in the hotel in September 1988. Directed by Mike Palmer, the Alan Ayckbourn comedy had a cast of seven which included Laurie Mansfield, Greg Greenhalgh, Sheila Freeman, Sylvia Pauline, Jill Musto and Mike Ames.

CADS rounded off 1988 with Peter Shaffer's **Black Comedy** which had a two-night run in the Globe Hotel and a final night at Rosehill Theatre. The show featured Nick Stanley, Charlotte Bevan, Richard Smithson, Stewart Grant, Mair Collins, Joan Hetherington, Alan Saunders and Des Mason. **Black Comedy** was co-directed by Liz Fitton and Len Wainwright and produced by Greg Greenhalgh.

△ *Marion Hughes* in the role of Abigail Williams in CADS 1988 production of **The Crucible**

△ The 1988 cast of CADS' **Can't Pay, Won't Pay**: *Heather Rogers, Alan Saunders, Jill Musto, Nick Stanley and Len Wainwright.*

1988

1989

1989

CADS' 1989 season opened in March with the World War I drama **Accrington Pals**. A party from the Carlisle based branch of the Western Front Association came to see the play and one of the group returned with his wife to see the play for a second time during its four nights' run in the Globe Hotel. Also in the audience was a gentleman called Pip Riley who had travelled from Garstang in Lancashire to see the show. Pip's grandfather, Harry Chapman, was one of the few survivors of the famous Accrington Pals battalion. The Times and Star newspaper review said, '*the ten strong cast gave totally convincing performances which would not have been out of place on the professional stage.*' The play starred Liz Fitton, Jill Musto, Neil McGurk and Trevor Wilson and was produced and directed by Greg Greenhalgh.

Bob and Liz Pritchard returned to the Quakers' Pardshaw Hall in April 1989 to stage Bertolt Brecht's humorous, yet sad tragedy, **Mother Courage**. Liz Pritchard directed a strong cast of twelve with Mary Coote in the title role. The play was performed for four nights on an open stage and producer, Bob Pritchard, provided a poignant backdrop to the play with projected period pictures of conflicts and photos of modern wars. CADS production of **Mother Courage** was runner up in the 1989 Cumbria Drama Awards.

Stewart Grant made his directorial debut for CADS in June 1989 with his production of Alan Bennett's **Habeas Corpus**. The comedy featured Lynette Norris (Mrs Swabb), Richard Smithson (the lecherous Dr Arthur), Sylvia Pauline, Joan Hetherington, Mike Ames, Alan Saunders, (Canon Throbbing), Charlotte Bevan, Des Mason, Jill Musto and Nick Stanley. **Habeas Corpus** played to capacity audiences for two nights in the Globe Hotel, followed by a final night at the Rosehill Theatre.

1989

△ CADS 1989 cast photo **Mother Courage**
L-R: *Paul Adams, Keith Irving, Sheila Freeman, Len Wainwright, Steward Grant, Joan Hetherington, Steve Barker, Mike Ames, Mike Palmer, Mary Coote, Marion Hughes* and *Laurie Mansfield.*

△ Cast photo **Habeas Corpus** 1989 L-R standing: *Des Mason, Mike Ames, Alan Saunders, Nick Stanley, Joan Hetherington, Charlotte Bevan* and *Richard Smithson.* Seated: *Lynette Norris, Sylvia Pauline,* and *Jill Musto.*

1989

△ *Neil McGurk* and *Keith Irving* in **Dumb Waiter** 1989

Next up, another new CADS director, Alan Saunders, cleverly designed a claustrophobic, stark set for **The Dumb Waiter** in the middle of the Globe Hotel ballroom and surrounded it with steeply-banked audience seating. The Times and Star newspaper described the acting of Keith Irving and Neil McGurk in **The Dumb Waiter** as '*masterly performances, which brought the characters to life*'.

Finally, in December 1989, Liz Fitton directed CADS 'play within a play' the **Farndale Avenue Housing Estate Townswomen's Guild Dramatic Society presentation of A Christmas Carol**. The cast of five were: Joan Hetherington, Jayne Bendall, Jill Musto, Pat Redmound and Greg Greenhalgh. Falling scenery, mistimed cues and

constant interruptions over the sound system kept the capacity audiences entertained for three nights in the Globe Hotel, followed by a final night at the Rosehill Theatre. Len Wainwright again produced the show – making it three in a row in 1989!

△ *Joan Hetherington, Jayne Bandall, Jill Musto, Pat Redmound* and *Greg Greenhalgh* in **Farndale Avenue 'A Christmas Carol'** 1989

1990

In 1990 CADS staged three full-length productions, a youth production and a Christmas Revue.

In March 1990, Greg Greenhalgh and Joan Hetherington produced and directed Robert Bolt's **A Man For All Seasons** at the Globe Hotel. Starring Laurie Mansfield as Sir Thomas More, the production also featured Paul Adams, Jim Bruce, Keith Irving, Sylvia Paulin, Elaine Kemball, Syd Wilcox, Mike Palmer, Bob Pritchard, Mike Ames, Trevor Wilson, Stewart Grant, Liz Fitton and Nick West. The production again won the Cumbria Drama Award for CADS for the best adult drama in the county in 1990.

In April Laurie Mansfield produced and directed **Animal Farm** at All Saints' School. His production was

the first CADS full-scale youth drama and used the talents of many pupils from Cockermouth School, who missed their school production that year because of rebuilding work on the school site. The cast of over thirty children were disguised in foam masks, manufactured in a number of workshops with the help of Ali McGaw. Music for the performance was directed by Sarah Ames.

▷ *Laurie Mansfield* and *Syd Wilcox* in a scene from **A Man For All Seasons** 1990

In June Bob Pritchard produced and directed the Alan Ayckbourn comedy **A Chorus of Disapproval,** a play based on a hapless Amdram society (C.A.O.S.) attempting to stage the Beggars' Opera. Richard Smithson gave a memorable portrayal of the manic director whose children had replaced him at home with a giant teddy bear (*'because daddy's never at home'*). Trevor Wilson played the role of the bit-part actor given the walk-on part of 'Crook-fingered Jack', but ends up taking the leading part.

1990

▷ *Jill Musto, Trevor Wilson* and *Jayne Bendall* in a scene from **A Chorus of Disapproval** 1990

In October 1990, Jill Musto and Richard Roper (assisted by Jayne Bendall) staged the black comedy **Rose** by Andrew Davis. The cast of eight were: Keith Irving, Elaine Kemball, Liz Fitton, Len Wainwright, Lynette Norris, Nick Stanley, Joan Hetherington and Joan Munro. Then just before Christmas 1990, CADS staged an **Old Time Music Hall** revue at the Globe Hotel.

With the closure of The Sportsman pub on Kirkgate, CADS had to find a new home for rehearsals and started using the upper-floor room in the Tithe Barn on Station Street.

◁ *Keith Irving, Elaine Kemball, Liz Fitton, Len Wainwright, Lynette Norris, Nick Stanley, Joan Hetherington* and *Joan Munro* in **Rose**. 1990

1990

1991

CADS's touring productions reached their peak in 1991, with three of their four productions that year, staged at the Globe Hotel, Keswick's Blue Box Theatre and Whitehaven's Rosehill. The fourth production, CADS first musical, **Jesus Christ Superstar**, launched a new theatrical venue in Cockermouth, Mitchell's Auction Rooms in Station Street!

In March 1991, CADS repeated their 1990 success and again won the Cumbria Drama Award with their production of the John Osborne classic, **Look Back In Anger**. Directed by Stewart Grant and produced by Greg Greenhalgh, **Look Back In Anger** starred Neil McGuirk as Jimmy Porter, the original 'angry young man', with memorable supporting roles from Joan Hetherington, Trevor Wilson, Richard Smithson and Elaine Kemball. Michael Hunter played a Miles Davis style trumpet backing to the scene changes. It had a period set designed by Keswick's Tony Doughty, (based on the original 1950s Royal Court Theatre production) with extensive, authentic props. **Look Back In Anger** toured theatres in Cockermouth, Keswick and Whitehaven.

△ *Elaine Kemball* and *Joan Hetherington* in **Look Back In Anger** 1991

1991

In May 1991, Nick Stanley's production of Shakespeare's **Twelfth Night** toured theatres in Cockermouth, Keswick and Whitehaven. The eighteen-strong cast included Lynette Norris as Viola, Stewart Grant as Orsino, Paul Adams as the Captain, Corrina Godfrey as Maria, Dave Stockwin as Sir Toby, Laurie Mansfield as Sir Andrew, Keith Irving as Feste, Richard Smithson as Malvolio, Trevor Wilson as Sebastian and Bob Pritchard as Antonio. The music for the show was composed by Cockermouth's Sara Kekus and the lavish costumes were hired from the Royal Shakespeare Company in Stratford.

Greg Greenhalgh assembled a cast of sixty-two from various Cumbria Youth Theatre groups to stage CADS' first rock opera in September 1991.

Mitchell's Auction was chosen as the venue for his production of the Andrew Lloyd-Webber / Tim Rice spectacular, **Jesus Christ Superstar**. Liz Fitton directed Trevor Wilson in the title role with Simon Thomas as Judas and Keri Whitehead as Mary. Keith Fitton provided the orchestration, with music direction by Mike Ames. Gill Palmer and Lynette Norris created original choreography for the show.

Then in November, Bob and Liz Pritchard staged their production of **The Government Inspector** at the Globe Hotel and the Rosehill Theatre. The play had a large cast of twenty-two actors with Nick Stanley in the title role. Dave Stockwin played the town Mayor with Joan Hetherington as his wife. Frank Higgins and Joe Blackadder

teamed up as two, larger-than-life, County Councillors.

1991

1991

Dave Stockwin, Frank Higgins, Joe Blackadder and *Roger Hopcroft* in **The Government Inspector** 1991

△ Cast photo **Sheep** 1992

1992

CADS probably had their most productive year in 1992 with no fewer than six full-scale, theatrical productions.

In January, CADS actor Richard Smithson penned his own script and the world premier of **Sheep** was staged at the Globe Hotel and at the Rosehill Theatre. Laurie Mansfield directed and Chris George produced the satirical piece, which featured Arabella Mansfield, Greg Greenhalgh, Beryl Balance, Mike Palmer, Joe Blackadder, Lin and Philip Malcolm and Corrina Godfrey in the principal parts. The 'sheep' were played by Jenni George, Sarah Warner, Jilly Terry and Siobhan Myres.

◁ *Yvonne Banham, Len Wainwright, Tracy Walker, Keith Irving, Alan Saunders* and *Joan Hetherington* in **Measure for Measure** 1992

1992

In April, Nick Stanley directed Shakespeare's **Measure for Measure.** Richard Smithson played the Duke of Vienna, Mike Palmer (Angelo) and Lynette Norris (Isabella). The show toured Whitehaven's Rosehill Theatre and Keswick's Blue Box Theatre as well as the Globe Hotel in Cockermouth.

Two months later, Trevor Wilson directed and Mike Ames produced Alan Ayckbourn's **Living Together**. Lynette Norris helped Trevor to put together a strong cast which included CADS stalwarts Joan Hetherington, Stewart Grant, Liz Fitton and Greg Greenhalgh. Dave Stockwin stole the show with his '*rangy and expressive*' performance as Reg, the board-game inventor. The comedy played to full houses in the Globe Hotel and the Blue Box.

1992

△ *Sharon Dobson* and *Greg Greenhalgh* in a scene from Ayckbourn's **Living Together** 1992

1992

Greg Greenhalgh, Liz Fitton and Mike Ames revived their 1991 musical **Jesus Christ Superstar** in the Spring of 1992, with Mike Palmer replacing Trevor Wilson as Jesus and Mike Stewart replacing Keith Irving as Pilot. The production team made an exploratory visit to Cockermouth's twin town of Marvejols to recruit thirty-two French teenagers and teach them the music and dance. Then this revived production was staged at the Workington Carnegie Theatre at the end of July and in Marvejols, France, in August, with a cast of both English and French actors.

In October, Nick Stanley directed and Cathy Avery produced Samuel Beckett's avant-garde classic, **Waiting for Godot**. Len Wainwright and Dave Stockwin played Vladimir and Estragon, supported by Frank Higgins, Geoff Hall and Ben Lanigan. The show was not staged in Cockermouth and played two nights only at Rosehill Theatre.

Finally, in December, Len Wainwright and Greg Greenhalgh directed and produced **The Killing of Sister George** at the Globe Hotel and at the Rosehill Theatre in Whitehaven. Liz Fitton and Marion Hughes played the leading roles, made famous by Beryl Reid and Susannah York in the 1970 film version. Sylvia Pauline played Madam Xenin and Cathy Avery made her acting début as a ruthless BBC executive.

1993

Stewart Grant, broke further new ground for CADS in February 1993, when he staged his production of **On the Razzle** at the Stanwix Arts Theatre in Carlisle. Not daunted by the prospect of touring with an extensive box set (designed by Wendy Haslam), Stewart's production attracted a large audience at the Stanwix, as well as full houses at the Globe Hotel in Cockermouth and the Rosehill Theatre in Whitehaven. The show had a large cast of twenty-three and an equally impressive 'road crew' of thirteen. Mike Palmer starred along with Joe Blackadder, Keith Irving and Chris Smith.

Following the success of the youth rock musical **Jesus Christ Superstar**, Lynette Norris assembled another exuberant,

Stage Manager, *Kate Brindle* in the dressing room at the Carnegie Theatre with *Simon Thomas, Keith Irving* with *Sam Dockwray* **Dracula Spectacula** 1993.

1993

young cast in May 1993 and staged the flamboyant musical, **Dracula Spectacula** at Workington's Carnegie Theatre. Keith Irving played the title role, with Sam Dockwray (Countess Wraith), Marie Bell (Miss Nadia Naïve) Simon Thomas (Genghis) and, cast heartthrob, Scott Davidson (Prof. Nick Necrophiliac). The musical also featured Nick Stanley as Herr Hans, Joan Munro as Frau Gretel, Malcolm Minty as Landau and Matthew Roberts as Father O'Stake.

△ 'The Pretty Girls': *Jenni Crowley, Louise Baker* and *Katie Gentry* from the cast of **Dracula Spectacula** 1993

△ *Stewart Grant, Joe Blackadder* and *Mair Collins* in a scene from **Death of a Salesman** 1993

In May 1993, Frank Higgins created a contemporary setting for the Arthur Miller classic, **Death of a Salesman**. Bob Pritchard produced and directed the show, with Stewart Grant in the principal role. Mike Palmer played the drifter son (Biff), Chris Smith, the younger son (Hap), and Mair Collins played the devoted mother who struggled to keep the family together. The show was staged at the Globe Hotel and at the Rosehill Theatre.

Len Wainwright and Marion Hughes teamed up in the autumn of 1993 to stage another Dario Fo farce, **Accidental Death of an Anarchist.** The play was based on the death of Giuseppe Pinelli in 1969, who fell – or was thrown – from the fourth floor window of a Milan police station. Dave Stockwin played the maniac who outsmarts the dim-witted Inspector Bertozzo (played by Chris Smith) with Joan Hetherington as the investigative journalist, and Errol Nixon, Mike Ames and Malcolm Minty as the corrupt carabinieri. The play followed in the footsteps of **On the Razzle,** also performing on successive nights at no fewer than three venues: the Globe Hotel in Cockermouth, the Rosehill Theatre in Whitehaven and the Stanwix Arts Theatre in Carlisle.

The year was rounded off with a fund-raising charity cabaret, **The Glory of Love,** at the Hundith Hill Hotel, near Cockermouth. Jill Roper and Liz Fitton co-directed and organised. Richard Smithson wrote some of the sketches and Alan Block produced the music.

1993

△ *Dave Stockwin* as the maniac, impersonating a visiting judge, in **Accidental Death of an Anarchist** 1993

1994

Five full-scale productions were staged in 1994, three of which had a cast of over twenty actors! Len Wainwright directed two of the shows, produced another and acted in the remaining shows that he didn't either direct or produce!

The year opened with Stewart Grant's grisly production of Shakespeare's **Richard III**, involving a large cast of twenty three. Mike Palmer played the title role and, once again, the production was staged at the Globe Hotel, Rosehill Theatre and at the Stanwix Arts Centre in Carlisle. Keith Irving played the scheming Duke of Norfolk and Joan Hetherington, Queen Elizabeth. Other cast members included Joe Blackadder, Mair Collins, Bob Pritchard, Marion Hughes, Errol Nixon, Nick Stanley, Mike Ames, Mark Osborne, Greg Greenhalgh, Deborah Hawkes, Syliva Paulin, Morag Wainwright, David Malcolm, Richard Smithson and Jane Lloyd.

Al Whittaker made a gruesome prop of a severed head, complete with dangling veins. There was also a sort of medieval computer to help the audience keep score of the dead. Kate Brindle stage-managed, Phil Mackie was brought in to direct the fencing scenes, and Wendy Haslam teamed up with Ian Johnson to produce the set.

◁ *Mair Collins, Sylvia Paulin, Mike Palmer* and *Joan Hetherington* in **Richard III.** 1994

△ The cast of **Shakers** 1994: *Liz Fitton, Lynette Norris, Sam Dockwray* and *Marion Hughes.*

Richard III was followed in April by Nick Stanley's production of **Shakers**, originally performed by the Hull Truck Theatre Company in 1981. Like **Richard III**, **Shakers** was also performed at the Globe Hotel and at the Rosehill Theatre. Assisted by Corrina Godfrey, Nick Stanley directed the small cast of Liz Fitton, Marion Hughes, Lynette Norris and Sam Dockwray.

In July, Richard Roper produced three one-act plays, **The Two of Us** by Michael Frayn. These plays were again staged at the Globe Hotel and at Rosehill Theatre. The first of the three plays, **Mr Foot**, was directed by Gill Palmer and featured Richard Smithson and Sheila Freeman. The second couple, Corrina Godfrey and Mark Osborne were directed by Len Wainwright in **The New Quixote**. Jill Roper directed the final couple, Nick Stanley and Joan Hetherington in **Chinaman**. Keith Fitton made his acting début as the 'whistling milkman' who linked the three plays.

The Cockermouth Scout Centre became another 'first' venue for CADS in the autumn of 1994 when Liz and Keith Fitton teamed up with Musical Director, Mike Ames, to stage Willie Russell's hit, **Our Day Out**. This was yet another big cast production with no fewer than six 'adults' and twenty-two youngsters! Jill Roper, Alan Block, Malcolm Minty and Zoe Calvert played the teachers with Richard Monksteel, the bus driver, and Len Wainwright, the caretaker. The youngsters included Anthony Longridge, Tom Bell, Louise Baker, Rebecca Sweeney, Arabella Mansfield, Kate Green, Alex Block, Garath Johnston, Phillip Malcolm, Graham McClelland, Jon Palmer, Sammy Fitton, Katie Wing, Hannah Wainwright, Morag Wainwright, Ben Musto, Becky Musto, Kirsten Johnson, Kathy Barker, Kathryn Banks, Alison Messenger and Rosemary Terry.

The cast of **Our Day Out** 1994

1994 ended with an hilarious production of **What the Butler Saw** directed by Len Wainwright and produced by Gill Palmer. Richard Smithson played the part of the mad Dr. Prentice with Liz Fitton, Greg Greenhalgh, Carol Jamieson, Richard Monksteel and Stewart Grant. Rehearsals for the show were held in Lloyd's car showroom on Low Road in Cockermouth!

▷ *Richard Smithson, Liz Fitton, Greg Greenhalgh, Carol Jamieson, Richard Monksteel* and *Stewart Grant* in **What the Butler Saw** 1994

1994

△ *Len Wainwright, Keith Fitton, Richard Smithson,*
Errol Nixon and *Al Whittaker* in **Much Ado About Nothing** 1995

1995

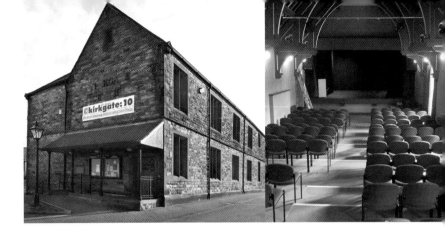

In the early 1970s, the need for a civic centre in Cockermouth was identified, but the difficulty of finding a suitable, affordable building remained an obstacle for a further two decades. At the beginning of 1990 Allerdale Council announced that it was going to demolish the unused, former All Saints' School in Kirkgate, Cockermouth. Opened in 1887, opposite the church of the same name, the school had stood empty for a number of years and when its demolition seemed inevitable, Cockermouth Civic Trust saw the opportunity they had been waiting for. After much negotiation, the building was acquired by them in 1993 and handed over to a newly-established, independent trust called the Kirkgate Centre Trust. Local retired architect, Peter Colley,

and his wife, Barbara were the driving force behind the Kirkgate Centre project, and on 24th January 1995 the new theatre opened its doors to the public.

On the opening night, CADS staged Shakespeare's **Much Ado About Nothing**, with a large cast of twenty-four players, starring Lynette Norris as the fiery Beatrice and Keith Irving as Benedick. The show was directed by Liz Pritchard and produced by her husband, Bob. After performing four nights to packed audiences in Cockermouth, the show's final night was staged at the Rosehill Theatre in Whitehaven.

A further four productions were staged in 1995, three of which were performed at the new Kirkgate Centre. In July, Nick Stanley directed

My Mother Said I Never Should, a four-handed drama featuring Rebecca Sweeney, Sam Dockwray, Jill Roper and Joan Munro.

In September, Corrina Godfrey starred in Willy Russell's single-handed comedy, **Shirley Valentine**. The show was produced and directed by Mike Palmer, who staged the play's final night at the Rosehill Theatre after a two-night run at the Kirkgate Centre.

In the winter months, Alan Block, Jackie Burd, Liz Fitton, Greg Greenhalgh, Gill Palmer, Richard Roper and Richard Smithson, designed and produced a musical comedy review, **Laughing Away**

The Pain, at the Kirkgate Centre. The theatre was converted to resemble a department store at Christmas and many of the sketches were written by Richard Smithson.

Director Len Wainwright, broke new ground again for CADS in 1995 when he staged Dario Fo's satire **Trumpets and Raspberries** at the newly opened Sheep and Wool Exhibition Centre on the outskirts of Cockermouth. The play had a cast of ten and starred Richard Monksteel, Richard Smithson, Joan Hetherington and Liz Chapman. The show's final night was staged in the comfort of Whitehaven's Rosehill Theatre.

1995

1996

In the summer of 1996, CADS made their début at the Edinburgh Fringe Festival. Richard Smithson had written the play, **Willy Nilly**, which was premièred at the Scout Centre in Cockermouth. Lynette Norris directed, Len Wainwright produced and the cast included Jill Roper, Sarah Warner, Liz Fitton, Gareth Douglas, Kevin Dempster, Len Wainwright, Errol Nixon and Nick Stanley.

Earlier in the year, Dave Stockwin had played the title role in Peter Shaffer's **Amadeus** alongside Keith Irving and Sam Dockwray. Produced and directed by Stewart Grant, the show was staged at the Kirkgate Centre and at the Rosehill Theatre.

In June 1996, Laurie Mansfield produced and directed **Jeffrey Bernard is Unwell** at the Kirkgate Centre. Dave Stockwin once again played the title role, with Liz Fitton, Richard Smithson, Greg Greenhalgh, Joan Hetherington and Rebecca Sweeney doubling into multi-characters.

Finally, in 1996, Bob and Liz Pritchard produced and directed Ben Jonson's comedy **The Alchemist** at the Kirkgate Centre and at the Rosehill Theatre. The show starred Stewart Grant, Joan Hetherington and Mike Palmer.

▷ *Stewart Grant, Joan Hetherington* and *Mike Palmer* in **The Alchemist** 1996

1996

1997

In the summer of 1997, Laurie Mansfield produced and directed the Ibsen play **Hedda Gabler** at the Kirkgate Centre. Sam Dockwray was cast in title role, supported by Joan Munro, Jackie Burd, Mike Palmer, Nicola Woodier, Mike Ames and Stewart Grant.

Jill and Richard Roper staged the Willy Russell comedy, **One For The Road**, at the Kirkgate Centre in November 1997. Iris Walton in the Times & Star said: '*Dave Stockwin gave a magnificent performance as Deninis Cain, the wannabe-twenty-again, with Liz Fitton turning in an equally fine performance as his less-than-confident-but-trying-hard wife…. CADS have done Willy Russell proud. I came away from the Kirkgate exhilarated and still laughing.*'

△ Cast photo **Hedda Gabler** 1997

△ **One For The Road** Director, *Jill Roper* (bottom left) with the cast: *Liz Fitton, Dave Stockwin, Joan Hetherington* and *Stewart Grant*. In the background are the stage managers, *Joan Munro* and *Jackie Burd*. 1997

1997

1998

Jan Dockwray made her CADS directorial début in March 1998 with a lavish production of **The Cherry Orchard** at the Kirkgate Centre. Dave Stockwin headed a sixteen-strong cast which included Joan Hetherington as Ranyevskaya and Stewart Grant as Lophakin. Bob Pritchard produced the show.

1998

◁ *Kerry Thornton* (Anya) with *Dave Stockwin* (Gayev) and *Jill Roper* (Varya) in a scene from **The Cherry Orchard** 1998

△ **Daisy Pulls It Off** 1998

Jill Roper and Liz Fitton combined to produce a cabaret, **For One Night Only**, at the Kirkgate Centre in July, which was followed in September, by Bob Pritchard's production of **Daisy Pulls It Off** at the Centre. The predominantly female cast of sixteen in **Daisy Pulls It Off** was led by Lynette Norris, Liz Fitton and Joan Hetherington.

Finally in 1998, Greg Greenhalgh produced and directed the musical play, **Whistle Down The Wind**. The forty-four strong cast was led by 17 year-old Nicola Barton, whom the Times & Star described as '*truly outstanding.*' She played the part of Cathy, made famous by Hayley Mills in the Richard Attenborough and Brian Forbes 1961 film version. Her siblings were played by 16 year-old Joelle Kemp and 13 year-old Jonathan Cuthel.

Chris George played the part of the escaped convict whom the children innocently believed to be Jesus Christ.

Revolving scenery was created for the set and much of the action was staged through the audience. Ann Dickens adapted and directed the complex musical score and the production played to packed houses all week at the Kirkgate Centre.

▷ *Chris George, Nicola Barton, Joelle Kemp* and *Jonathan Cuthel* in **Whistle Down The Wind** 1998

1998

1999

Len Wainwright once again took over the director's chair in March 1999 and staged the Pinter classic, **The Homecoming**, at the Kirkgate Centre and in the new Rosehill Barn Theatre in Whitehaven. The six strong cast were Morgan Sweeney, Chris George, Stewart Grant, Rosie Beeby, Dave Stockwin and Matthew Roberts. John Wright, writing in the Times & Star, said: 'Cockermouth Amateur Dramatic Society should have provided counselling as part of the ticket price. So gripping was the group's performance, the audience was visibly moved by the experience.'

Bob and Liz Pritchard assembled a twenty-three strong cast to stage Shakespeare's **A Midsummer Nights Dream (Le Songe D'Une Nuit D'Eté)** at the Kirkgate Centre in Cockermouth, then 1,000 miles south in Cockermouth's twin town, Marvejols in France. Principal roles were played by Dave Malcolm (Oberon), Sandra Matitia (Titania), Ed Farrell (Lysander), Phil Malcolm (Demetrius), Lucy Gunson (Helena), Jenny Thornton (Hermia), Judith Windsor (Puck) and Joe Blackadder (Narrator and the character, Peter Quince).

Len Wainwright then directed Joe Orton's black comedy, **Entertaining Mr Slone**, in November 1999. A stylised set was designed and constructed by Frank Higgins and the show featuring Roy Blackburn, Stewart Grant, Debbie Austin and Greg Greenhalgh was performed at the Kirkgate Centre, in the new Keswick Studio Theatre at the Theatre by the Lake and at the Rosehill Theatre.

△ *Morgan Sweeney, Chris George, Stewart Grant, Rosie Beeby, Dave Stockwin* and *Matthew Roberts* in **The Homecoming** 1999

△ **A Midsummer Night's Dream** performed in Marvejols, France in 1999.' The 'Mechanicals' were *Chris George* (Mur) and behind the 'wall', *Frank Higgins* (Bottom playing Pyramus) and *Greg Greenhalgh* (Clair de lune)

1999

*Roy Blackburn, Stewart Grant,
Debbie Austin* and *Greg Greenhalgh*
in **Entertaining Mr Slone** 1999

2000

In the January of the new millennium, CADS producer, Chris George, staged three Alan Bennett monologues at the Kirkgate Centre. Rosie Beeby directed **Graham** played by Frank Higgins. Jill Roper played **Susan** directed by Liz Fitton and Sandra Matitia and Laurie Mansfield directed Joan Hetherington in **Irene**.

In March, Greg Greenhalgh produced and directed a new stage-play adaptation of the Charlotte Bronte classic, **Jane Eyre**. Written by Willis Hall, the play had a huge cast of thirty-five actors, including ten children. With such a large cast, Greg designed the show to be played 'in the round' using much of the floor area of the Kirkgate Centre. Tiered seating was erected around the performing area and onto the actual stage.

Lucy Gunson played the title role of **Jane Eyre** with Stewart Grant as Edward Rochester. The Times & Star review said: '*Lucy Gunson is outstanding as Bronte's plain but spirited orphan girl …. she captures well Jane Eyre's vulnerability.*' Of Stewart Grant's performance the newspaper said: '*Stewart Grant is superb as Rochester*'.

▷ The poster for **Jane Eyre** 2000 featuring *Lucy Gunson* as Jane Eyre

CADS
Cockermouth Amateur
Dramatic Society

Charlotte Brontë's

Jane Eyre

A new stage adaptation of the timeless classic by **Willis Hall**

8.00 pm
Wednesday - Saturday,
March 1st - 4th
Kirkgate Centre
Cockermouth
Tickets £5/£3
from the Ticket Office
01900 826448
or Kovary's
01900 822314

supported by **R. LLOYD MOTORS LTD**

Jane Eyre was followed in July with **A View from the Bridge** by Arthur Miller. Directed by Frank Higgins and produced by Bob Pritchard, **A View from the Bridge** had a four night run at the Kirkgate Centre with a cast of eleven. The Times & Star headline read, *'amateurs show an absolutely brilliant view from the bridge … brilliant, absolutely brilliant!'* The principal character, Eddie Carbone, was played by Mike Palmer with Corrina Godfrey as his wife Beatrice. Alice Bate played their daughter, Catherine, with Dominic Hughes and Ed Farrell as the Italian pair, Rodolpho and Marco. Stewart Grant played the narrator/lawyer, Alfieri.

2000

▷ *Stewart Grant* as the narrator /lawyer, Alfieri in **A View from the Bridge**

Then in October 2000, Nick Stanley directed **Death and the Maiden** at the Kirkgate Centre with Julie Skidmore, Roy Blackburn and Stewart Grant in this 'edge of the seat', Ariel Dorfman thriller. Nick's design for the show had the audience seated on the stage looking down onto the action into an auditorium cleverly shrouded in black curtains. Kevin Pearson, writing in the Times & Star, said: *'Nick Stanley must be commended for bringing out such performances from his three main actors. Julie Skidmore played with authenticity and her emotional delivery and haunted face evoked the unthinkable horrors of her past, giving the impression that she was in fact a woman close to breaking'.*

In the autumn of 2000, Bob Pritchard set up a CADS touring company called the 'A595 Theatre Company' which performed the J.B. Priestley comedy **When We Are Married** in village halls in Fletchertown, Dean, Kirkbampton, Plumbland, Rosely, St.Bees and Ravenglass as well as on the stage at the Kirkgate Centre and in the studio theatre at Keswick's Theatre by the Lake. The play had a cast of fourteen, starring Laurie Mansfield as the endearingly, stuttering Herbert Soppitt and Mary Coote as his sharp-tongued wife.

▷ The programme cover for CADS
Death and the Maiden 2000

CADS present
Cockermouth Amateur
Dramatic Society

DEATH and the MAIDEN
by Ariel Dorfman
KIRKGATE CENTRE COCKERMOUTH
10th to 14th October 2000

2000

△ *Hannah Evans* and *Donald Renouf*
in **When We Are Married** 2000

2000

Beyond 2000

Into a new century and a new millennium, CADS continued the tradition of over a hundred years of live theatre in Cockermouth.

Throughout the first decade of the new century, CADS founder, Bob Pritchard, continued his 'A595' village hall tours, with **Blithe Spirit** in 2002, **How The Other Half Loves** in 2005, **Absolute Turkey** in 2007 and **Noises Off** in 2010.

In 2005 the Kirkgate Centre celebrated its 10th Anniversary, maintaining a year-round programme of live entertainment. In 2009 CADS marked their 25th Anniversary, still staging two or three productions every year

and now including an annual children's pantomime.

The curtain may have come down on the last show but rehearsals are already under way for the next production.